I HEART

PACIFIC NORTHWEST

Memorable Backcountry Meals

44 RECIPES WORTH MAKING

by Lisa "Deepdive" Holmes & Sanjana "Spice Girl" Sachdeva

Design by Lisa D. Holmes (yulanstudio.com)

Photographs by Lisa D. Holmes & Sanjana Sachdeva

Published in Portland, Oregon, by Yulan Studio, Inc.

Printed in the United States.

First edition

ISBN 978-0-9915382-8-7

Contents

About the Authors

We're both graphic designers based in Portland, Oregon, who met while doing volunteer work for a local design association. We've been going on outdoor adventures together for over ten years, and when we got started backpacking, we didn't like the commercial food choices that were available. We're both picky eaters who prefer fresh, local and organic foods whenever possible, so we decided to start making our own backpacking meals. Over the years, our friends sampled our food on trips and encouraged us to develop this cookbook. Between the two of us, we offer a mix of comfort foods and spicier meal options.

LISA "DEEPDIVE" HOLMES is a graphic designer, hiking book author and blogger. When she's not designing websites and marketing materials for clients, she's "diving deep" into the details of planning backpacking trips all over the beautiful Pacific Northwest. Learn more about her hiking books and follow her adventures at iheartpacificnorthwest.com.

SANJANA "SPICE GIRL" SACHDEVA is a graphic designer and photographer. When she's not hiking or backpacking, she utilizes spices from around the world to create meals using seasonal ingredients. Her passion for photography takes her to beautiful places in the Pacific Northwest, where she creates images that convey peace and harmony. Learn more about her photography at sanjana-sachdeva.com.

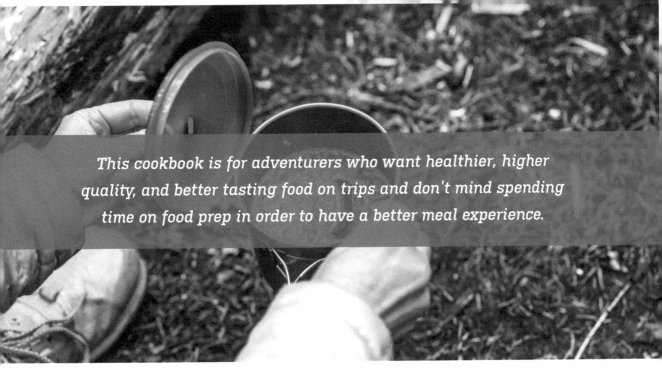

This cookbook is for adventurers who want healthier, higher quality, and better tasting food on trips and don't mind spending time on food prep in order to have a better meal experience.

About this Cookbook

WHY MAKE YOUR OWN BACKPACKING MEALS?

Preparing your own meals allows you to control the quality of ingredients, eliminating the additives and preservatives found in most commercial meals. It also allows you to customize the flavor and dietary needs of meals to your own preference. We prefer to use organic ingredients and take advantage of home gardens to dehydrate surplus vegetables. It's all up to you!

DEHYDRATING INGREDIENTS

Most of the recipes in this cookbook require the use of a dehydrator, although many dried ingredients can be purchased instead. The recipes also make use of some specialized ingredients (such as butter powder, milk powder, and cheese powder) that need to be purchased since it's not feasible to make your own. We provide a list of our favorite resources for these items.

PREP AT HOME, NOT AT CAMP

The recipes in this cookbook are based on packaging dried foods for cooking with little to no prep done at camp. This saves time and allows for using minimal kitchen gear on trips. There's no need for a cutting board, cooking utensils, or additional cookware... just a backpacking stove and spoon (or spork). Backpacking is hard enough and we want meals that are easy to prepare once we are at camp.

COOKING IN A POT VERSUS REHYDRATING IN A BAG

The majority of recipes in this cookbook are best prepared in a pot on a backpacking stove. While most commercial backpacking meals are prepared by adding boiling water to the bag, cooking in a pot allows you to refine the cooking process for better results. Preparing meals this way helps to ensure that everything is thoroughly cooked, doesn't have too much liquid, and is still hot when you eat it. In addition, you aren't left with a messy and smelly plastic bag in your camp trash. We would rather spend a small amount of time doing cleanup in order to get an overall better meal experience.

COLD SOAK OPTIONS

Not every meal needs to be cooked in order to be full of flavor. In this cookbook, we offer five cold soak recipes that work great for lunches. Just add cold water and let them soak while you hike.

HOW NUTRITION INFO WAS DETERMINED

We used an online calculator to determine the nutritional info for each recipe. While we strived to get accurate data, the nutritional values will vary based on the ingredients used, so the info provided is a general guideline.

Dehydrating Basics

Not only is dehydrating your own ingredients a great way to save money on backpacking food, it's also a good method for controlling the quality of the items used in meals – as well as being able to tailor the taste of meals to your preferences.

TYPES OF DEHYDRATORS

When purchasing a dehydrator, there are many options to consider, including the type of dehydrator, features to consider, and overall cost.

If you are just getting started and don't want to spend a lot, a round dehydrator with stacking trays is a good option. For this type of dehydrator, we recommend the Nesco brand. On most round dehydrators, the fan is located on the top, so the trays may need to be rotated during the drying process. Feature options include digital temperature and timer controls, and fans with varying wattages.

We both used lower cost, round dehydrators for several years but eventually upgraded to Excalibur

brand dehydrators. We needed to be able to dry larger quantities of foods, and the square-shaped Excalibur trays hold more food than the round-style trays, as well as being easier to load and unload. In addition, we feel that the overall quality of dried food is much better with this brand. The fan is located on the back of the unit, which allows for more even food drying, and rotating the trays is usually not necessary.

However, a lower cost dehydrator will be able to do a good job, so choose what works best for your budget.

As far as features go, we look for models with temperature control, preferably including a range from 95 degrees (best for delicate herbs and greens) to 155 degrees (best for jerky and meats). Unless you need a timer to be able to turn the unit off at a certain time, this feature is not as useful since drying times vary greatly based on many variables.

Silicone or plastic tray liners (also called fruit roll sheets) are highly recommended for drying foods with sauces or that have small pieces that could fall through open or mesh trays. We use these for most of the ingredients that we dehydrate.

TYPES OF FOOD THAT DEHYDRATE WELL

Fruit, vegetables, beans, pasta, grains, rice, and lean meats can all be dehydrated at home. Fresh fruit and vegetables can be dehydrated cooked or raw, while beans, pasta, grains, rice, and meats will need to be cooked first, then dehydrated.

FOODS THAT AREN'T SUITABLE FOR DEHYDRATING

Foods with a higher fat content (including milk, cheese, avocado, and fatty meats) will tend to go rancid quickly so we recommend purchasing freeze-dried products for these types of ingredients instead. See the Sourcing Ingredients section for more info on where to purchase.

FOOD PREPARATION

Cut ingredients into small, uniform-size pieces for the best results. To save time, pre-cut canned or frozen foods also work well for dehydrating.

Spread ingredients evenly on dehydrator trays, preventing overlapping and leaving space around items for better drying. For sauces, spread onto a silicone or plastic tray evenly in a thin layer using a spatula.

DRYING TIMES

The amount of time it takes for ingredients to dehydrate can vary widely based on many variables, including: the humidity and temperature of the room; whether the food is fresh, canned or frozen; the size and shape of cut ingredients; and the type of dehydrator used.

Instead of listing times for dehydrating ingredients, we recommend drying food in the dehydrator until it is completely dry. This process can take anywhere from 4 hours to over 12 hours, and often means leaving the dehydrator running overnight. Since over-drying is not an issue, it's better to dry food for longer timeframes versus under-drying and risking food safety.

STORING DEHYDRATED INGREDIENTS

Unless you plan to use the dehydrated ingredients right away, proper storage will lengthen the amount of time they will keep. Store in an airtight container, such as a heavy duty plastic bag with all of the air pushed out (for short term storage), vacuum-sealed bag, or glass canning jars. For longer term storage, add an oxygen absorber packet to the container, or use a vacuum-sealing jar attachment to create an airtight seal on mason-type jars. Store in a cool, dry location, or in the freezer.

Beans

black beans

chickpeas

navy beans

Pre-cook beans in a slow cooker, pressure cooker, or use canned beans. Beans should be fully cooked, but not mushy. Drain liquid before dehydrating. Beans will split when dehydrating, which allows them to rehydrate easier. Beans should be completely dry and hard after dehydrating.

Recommended temperature for dehydrating: 125 degrees
Approximate timeframe: 6-8 hours

Meat

chicken meatballs

beef meatballs

salmon

Lean meats dehydrate and store better than meats with fat, which can spoil or go rancid quickly. This cookbook includes recipes using homemade meatballs and canned salmon. For meatballs, cut into 6-8 pieces for better rehydration. For salmon, drain canned salmon (packed in water, not oil) and break into small pieces, then spread into a thin layer on dehydrator trays.

Recommended temperature for dehydrating: 155 degrees
Approximate timeframe: 6-8 hours

Pasta

egg noodles

macaroni

spaghetti

It may seem counterintuitive to cook and dehydrate pasta since it's already in dried form, but pasta that's been pre-cooked will take much less time and fuel to cook on trips.

Almost any type of pasta can be pre-cooked and dehydrated, but in general, we recommend using pasta that cooks in 8 minutes or less so it will rehydrate completely. Pasta should be fully cooked a few minutes past al dente but not mushy.

After cooking, drain the pasta and rinse with cold water to prevent sticking together. Spread into a thin layer on dehydrator trays, or for long noodles such as angel hair pasta or spaghetti, shape into small nests.

Recommended temperature: 125 degrees
Approximate timeframe: 4-6 hours

Rice

basmati rice

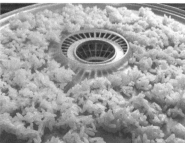
jasmine rice

risotto

While you could use instant rice in backpacking meals, it's more economical and provides better nutrition when you pre-cook and dehydrate rice at home. For most recipes, we recommend Indian Basmati rice for the texture – it doesn't clump or become sticky when rehydrated, unlike other types of white rice. The thinness of the grains makes rehydrating faster too. For creamy risotto, we pre-cook arborio rice in broth and spread thinly on dehydrator trays with a bit of the sauce.

Recommended temperature: 125 degrees
Approximate timeframe: 8-12 hours

Vegetables

artichoke hearts

broccoli

butternut squash

carrots

green onions

mushrooms

peppers

tomatoes

zucchini

Fresh or frozen vegetables work best for dehydrating. While canned vegetables in general don't work as well, there are a few exceptions such as capers, olives, artichoke hearts, and roasted red peppers – all of which are used in recipes in this cookbook.

Most vegetables are dehydrated raw, such as green onions, carrots, peas, mushrooms, tomatoes, and zucchini. Vegetables that need to be cooked or blanched first include potatoes, broccoli and winter squash. We like to purchase frozen fire-roasted onions and peppers for dehydrating.

Cut into uniform pieces or shred vegetables and spread in a thin layer on dehydrator trays.

Recommended temperature: 125 degrees
Approximate timeframe: 6-12 hours

Greens & Herbs

rosemary

kale

spinach

Greens and herbs are a great addition to backpacking meals. To dehydrate, choose fresh herbs or greens and leave on the stem for drying. Wash and pat dry before placing on dehydrator trays. After they are dry, strip the stems off and crush or break into small pieces for storing.

Recommended temperature: 95 degrees
Approximate timeframe: 2-6 hours

Fruit

apples

peaches

oranges

Dried fruit, used in this cookbook for breakfast and dessert recipes, also makes a great trail snack. Almost any type of fruit can be dehydrated, including apples, pears, bananas, peaches, berries, kiwi, melons and mango.

Fresh or frozen fruits can be dehydrated. For fresh fruits, choose ripe but not overly ripe or mushy fruit. Cut into thin slices or small pieces for better rehydration. To prevent browning, lightly coat cut fruit with lemon juice before dehydrating.

Recommended temperature: 125 degrees
Approximate timeframe: 8-12 hours

Sourcing Ingredients

While we prefer to dehydrate as many of the ingredients as possible that are used in these recipes, there are some dried ingredients that must be purchased, including:

+ butter, milk, sour cream, and heavy cream powders
+ cheese powder
+ freeze-dried shredded cheese
+ bacon jerky and other dried meat products
+ coconut milk powder
+ crystallized lemon and lime powders

We've provided a list on the next page of our preferred resources for these products. You may be able to find some of these items in local grocery stores, including bulk food sections, but most are only available online.

In addition, you could purchase dehydrated or freeze-dried fruits, vegetables and grains for use in recipes instead of dehydrating them yourself. The overall cost of the meals will be higher, but it will definitely save time.

When purchasing dried items, pay attention to the ingredients to avoid items with preservatives and artificial ingredients. We try to buy from smaller companies that specialize in preservative-free and organic options whenever possible.

One of our favorite stores for ingredients is Trader Joe's. We used all of these items in the recipes:

+ fire-roasted peppers and onions (frozen)
+ fire-roasted corn (frozen)
+ artichoke hearts (canned)
+ black olives (canned)
+ sun-dried tomatoes (not packed in oil)
+ various nuts and seeds
+ coconut oil (available in jars and individual packets)
+ freeze-dried berries
+ dried fruit
+ salmon (canned)
+ mushroom powder

ONLINE RESOURCES FOR INGREDIENTS

Anthony's Goods (anthonysgoods.com)
+ butter powder
+ heavy cream powder
+ cheese powder
+ coconut milk powder
+ almond protein powder

Bob's Red Mill (bobsredmill.com)
+ instant potato flakes
+ cornstarch and potato starch
+ dried beans and lentils

Harmony House (harmonyhousefoods.com)
+ vegetables (dehydrated and freeze-dried)
+ fruit (freeze-dried)
+ beans (dehydrated)

Meat Shredz (meatshredz.com)
+ dried pulled pork

Minimus (minums.biz)
+ travel size packets of condiments

Mother Earth Products (motherearthproducts.com)
+ beans (dehydrated)
+ vegetables (dehydrated and freeze-dried)
+ fruit (freeze-dried)

North Bay Trading Company (northbaytrading.com)
+ vegetables (dehydrated and freeze-dried)
+ fruit (freeze-dried)

Oberto (oberto.com)
+ dried meats and jerky

Packit Gourmet (packitgourmet.com)
+ vegetables (dehydrated and freeze-dried)
+ fruit (freeze-dried)
+ beans & grains (dehydrated)
+ cheese powders, egg powders, dairy powders
+ instant coffee, tea
+ condiments
+ crystallized lemon and lime powders

Savory Spice (savoryspiceshop.com)
+ high quality dried spices and seasoning mixes

Assembling & Storing Dehydrated Meals

ASSEMBLING MEALS

When you have all of your dehydrated ingredients ready to assemble into meals, save time by putting together multiple meals at once. We like to use a small container to stand the bags in for filling. This way, it's easier to put the ingredients into each bag one by one.

When using a vacuum sealer, mix together all of the dry ingredients so they don't clump together. This is especially helpful for powdered ingredients, but also helps coat sharper objects so they don't puncture the bag.

Keep ingredients with moisture separate, such as grated cheese, sun-dried tomatoes, or bacon jerky. Small plastic pill bags can be purchased in bulk online for this purpose.

For bringing liquids such as soy sauce or oils on trips, we like to use small plastic bottles with lids (1 fl. oz. Nalgene bottles work great for this).

VACUUM-SEALING MEALS

When storing assembled meals, we recommend using a vacuum sealer and storing meals in the freezer until needed for a trip. The vacuum-sealing process removes air from the package, reducing the chances for bacteria to grow. While regular plastic bags will do the job for short term storage, they aren't optimal for long term storage. Even when you push all of air out of them, they still aren't air-tight like vacuum sealed bags are. Vacuum sealing also helps to reduce odors in your food bag, and they take up less space.

When purchasing a vacuum-sealer, look for a model with a bag cutter for use with continuous rolls of vacuum seal material. We like to use 8-inch wide rolls instead of quart-size bags and cut the material to size. This helps to cut costs and reduces the overall amount of packaging used. Some vacuum sealers have an option to add a jar sealing kit for removing air from glass jars, handy for storing dried ingredients before assembling into meals.

Sharp food objects like rice or pasta have a tendency to pierce the bags, so place a paper towel on the inside of the bag before sealing to eliminate this problem. The paper towel can be used to wipe your pot clean after eating.

LABELING MEALS

Label meals with the name of the meal, date prepared, and instructions on how to prepare at camp. Address labels sold in office supply stores work well for this purpose, or use a permanent marker and write directly on the bag.

For example:

Almond Berry Oatmeal
September 2021
4 oz. water
simmer 2 min.
cover & soak 5 min.
add 1 TBS coconut oil

STORING MEALS

If you are using assembled meals within a few weeks, store them in food-grade plastic or mylar bags in a cool, dark location such as in a dark colored bin or in a closet. For longer term storage, we recommend storing meals in the freezer. Most meals will be shelf stable for six months, up to a year if kept in the freezer.

For trail bars, trail mix and other snacks, we like to use reusable plastic bags, such as the brand ReZip. Silicone bags work well too, but they are much heavier and bulkier.

PACKING MEALS FOR A TRIP

To prepare for a trip, keeping food organized by day or by type of meals will make it easier to find what you need. We like to use gallon-size odor proof bags for this purpose and package all breakfasts in one bag, lunches and snacks in another, and dinners together.

When we need to use a bear canister, we skip the step of organizing meals in gallon-size bags and pack everything into the canister separately. To fill, lay the canister on its side and place each meal vertically, then place smaller items in between meals. This helps to keep everything easily accessible without needing to empty the canister to find items.

Your body works hard to get you where you are going while backpacking, so it's important to provide it with enough calories, protein, healthy fats, and nutrients to sustain you.

Nutrition

It's essential to understand how the calories you eat fuel your trips since you'll burn more calories during a day of backpacking than on a normal day. How much you burn depends upon your body, the terrain, elevation, pack weight, and distance. And remember, not all calories are equal, so replenish yourself with a diverse mix of foods.

Carbohydrates provide the quickest energy and are the main focus of most backpacking meals. Simple sugar provides a quick energy burst, but grains, vegetables, beans and legumes provide complex carbs that supply longer-lasting energy. Protein sources, such as meat, eggs, dairy, whole grains, and legumes, are good for renewing muscles and body tissue. And healthy fats from nut butters, olive oil, or coconut oil can provide slow-burning energy needed by backpackers.

Meal Planning

The key to meal planning for backpacking is to bring food that is calorie dense and lightweight. Your food also needs to be appealing to eat, because it's not uncommon to experience a loss of appetite when you're tired from exertion. That is the reason this cookbook exists! We needed food we would actually want to eat on trips, so we developed these recipes.

HOW MUCH FOOD TO TAKE

You may have heard the general recommendation on how much food to bring, which is about 2 pounds of food per day. However, when you make your own dehydrated meals, they will typically weigh less than commercial meals (and take up much less space in your food bag).

Your approach to lunches will also have an impact on the weight of your food bag. If you are using the cold soak lunch recipes in this cookbook, they will weigh much less than typical backpacker lunch fare, such as tuna packets and tortillas.

And you may need fewer snacks (which tend to be heavy) if you have a trip menu with fulfilling meals that keep you satisfied.

Instead of relying on the weight of your food bag to ensure you have the correct amount, pay attention to the nutrition info, especially calories.

Adjust the amount of food needed based on trip exertion and duration: for shorter trips, take smaller, less caloric meals; for extended or strenuous trips, plan for larger high calorie meals.

CREATING A MENU PLAN

Consider the trip timeframe when planning a menu. Depending on when your trip starts and ends, you likely won't need to take breakfast for the first day or dinner for the last.

Also keep in mind what each day of a trip entails. For example, on days with strenuous hikes, you'll want meals that are simple to prepare. And on easier days, you're likely to have more energy for meals that take a bit more time to prepare. Or, maybe add in a dessert for an after dinner treat when you have more time to enjoy it.

Once you know how many and what types of meals you need, write a menu plan for each day of the trip. List what you'll take for each breakfast, lunch, and dinner, as well as snacks, beverages, and condiments.

Visualizing a trip menu is another good method for determining how much food you need. To do this, lay out all of the meals on a table or countertop in rows for each day. This way, you can see how much food you have for each meal – which will help make sure you're bringing enough but not too much. To determine the amount of snacks you'll need, package all of your snacks into individual bags – one for each day of a trip.

PLANNING FOR EMERGENCIES

It's always a good idea to add in a few extra trail bars or an additional meal for just in case. Sometimes trips are extended for reasons out of our control such as accidents or weather, and having food in these times can make a difference in our abilities to think clearly and keep energy levels up when needed.

KITCHEN GEAR

The recipes in this cookbook can all be prepared using minimal kitchen gear: a backpacking stove and fuel, a pot with a lid, and a spoon or spork.

BACKPACKING STOVES

Since the recipes in this cookbook are based on cooking in a pot (versus adding boiling water to a package), there are several features to keep in mind when purchasing a stove.

While there are many types of stoves to consider, we recommend canister or integrated canister stoves. When using alcohol or alternative fuel stoves, you can't control the level of heat and food burns much more easily.

Canister stoves are a popular choice for most backpackers due to being small, lightweight and easy to use. These stoves, which do not include a pan or other cookware, have been designed to take up minimal space, with pot supports that fold down when not in use.

Integrated canister stoves feature a burner that connects to a pot with heat exchangers on the bottom. Jetboil and MSR are two of the most popular stoves of this type. The heat exchanger makes integrated canister stoves more fuel efficient and wind resistant than regular canister stoves. Though they tend to be a bit heavier and bulkier, they are popular due to being the easiest to use of all types of backpacking stoves. Some models are meant for boiling water only and are not recommended for cooking food in, while other models feature the ability to control the temperature for simmering capability, so make sure you know what the stove is capable of before purchasing.

Burner heads on canister stoves vary in size and style. Some offer larger burners that work well for group cooking, while compact burners generally perform better with smaller lightweight pots. The shape of the burner head affects performance as well. For example, concave burner heads provide better wind resistance.

FUEL

Canister stoves run off of a pressurized blend of propane and butane or isobutane fuel, available at outdoor

retailers. Connect the stove to the fuel canister via a threaded valve, then set your pot on top of the stove supports. To light, use a lighter or look for a stove with a built-in piezo igniter. Models with this feature are lit by turning on the fuel, then pressing the piezo button which creates a spark to light the stove.

Tip: when empty, you can recycle fuel canisters by puncturing them. Make sure they are empty first, and use a crunch tool (available at outdoor retailers) to make the job easier.

COOKWARE & UTENSILS

Investing in a good quality pot with a lid can help make cooking at camp a better overall experience. You'll want a pot that can be handled safely while cooking, doesn't scorch food, and preferably, doesn't weigh down your pack.

Titanium pots are the lightest in weight and bulk, but you'll need to be careful to not burn when cooking since the thinner material conducts heat faster.

Aluminum pots are heavier but are more durable and maintain even heat while cooking.

Look for a lid that can be easily removed from a pot while cooking, as well as one that sits firmly on the pot. A nice to have feature on a lid is built-in drainage holes, helpful for straining liquids when needed.

Using a mug instead of your cook pot for hot drinks has several benefits: the drink won't be flavored by the last meal you ate, and it saves time since you can prepare a hot drink and a meal at the same time. For packability, look for a mug that can nest inside your cook pot. Instead of a plastic mug, consider using a small cook pot with folding handles for the benefit of being able to heat water directly in it as well as to have a backup for your main cooking pot.

For utensils, consider a longer handle spoon for stirring (and keeping your hand out of the heat) while cooking. Titanium spoons and sporks are a popular ultralight option that tend to last much longer than plastic.

BACKCOUNTRY FOOD STORAGE

Proper storage of food while backpacking is critical, not only for protecting your food, but also to make sure that wildlife doesn't become accustomed to looking for food from humans. Plan to store your food at least 200 feet (70 steps) from your camp.

If you don't store your food properly, you may attract wildlife to your campsite. Keeping food in a tent or on the ground near the tent is not recommended. Most people think of protecting food from bears, but small critters can be especially troublesome and will gnaw through backpacks and tents to get to food.

FOOD STORAGE GEAR

There are three main options for food storage in the backcountry: food sacks, bear bags, and bear canisters.

Food sacks, which need to be properly hung for food storage while backpacking, can be any type of bag that can hold your food and be fastened shut. A waterproof dry sack is a good option. Food sack kits are often sold with a carabiner and a small "rock" sack for throwing rope over a high branch.

Bear bags are made from a sturdy specialty fabric that bears can't tear into. They are a good option where bear canisters are not required. Instead of needing to hang high like a food sack, they can be tied around a tree or branch. There are several models available: bear-resistant, rodent-resistant, and a model that combines both types of material in one bag.

Odor-proof plastic bags are recommended for use in both food sacks and bear bags.

Bear canisters are hard-sided containers made from plastic or carbon fiber with lids that wildlife cannot open. They are the heaviest food storage option available, but they are also the easist to store and the most effective at keeping all types of wildlife from getting into your food. They are sold in various sizes so you can choose one based on the capacity needed.

Since you'll also need to store all scented items in your food bag or bear canister, make sure to purchase one large enough to hold everything.

WHERE TO STORE FOOD

Hanging food: Most places will require food to be hung. In bear country, the hang will need to be 15 feet off the ground and 8 feet away from the base of the tree. In areas where bears aren't an issue it is still necessary to do a critter hang, which can be at a lower height. Pans used for cooking food, bowls, plates, mugs, and utensils should all be hung with your food since they will likely hold onto food smells even after washing.

Bear protection: In some backcountry locations, such as national parks, bear canisters may be required for storage of food, trash, and scented items. Some ranger stations loan or rent bear canisters in areas where they are required. While bears may be able to retrieve and move a bear canister, they will not be able to get inside. Don't keep the canister in your tent. Instead, store it away from your campsite. Be careful about leaving it in a place where it could roll off a cliff or into a stream if knocked around by curious wildlife or clumsy campers.

Some backcountry campsites have tall poles or wire pulley systems for hanging food, or metal food lockers

for communal food storage. These are more common in heavy-use areas where bears are accustomed to looking for food. Be sure to use them when they are available.

FOOD PREPARATION

For meal preparation while backpacking, a separate kitchen location should be selected when possible. Kitchens serve the purpose of keeping food smells confined to a single area, and help to prevent animals, big and small, from being attracted to your sleeping location.

LOCATION OF CAMP KITCHEN

Backcountry kitchens and food storage areas should be set up no closer than 200 feet (about 70 steps) from water sources, and preferably at least 200 feet from your sleep area when possible. This is especially important in bear country. Many established campsites already have a place set up for cooking, with a fire ring and rocks or logs placed for sitting. If you need to create a camp kitchen area, an ideal location is on a durable surface such as bare ground or on rocks to help protect the surrounding environment.

FOOD PREPARATION

While heating your backcountry cuisine, be sure to place your stove on a level surface. Flat rocks work best when available. Many backcountry injuries result from a pot of boiling water falling off an unstable stove and burning the user. Follow the stove manufacturer's instructions to avoid accidental fires, fuel spillage, and other potential issues. And don't cook in your tent – using a stove in an enclosed area can put you in danger of both a fire and carbon monoxide poisoning.

CLEAN UP

All camp kitchen trash should be packed out. To cut down on the amount of packaging and food waste on trips, prepare at home by bringing properly sized meal portions, eliminating excess packaging materials, and repackaging foods sold in bulky bags or boxes. Food packaging should not be burned in a campfire due to the coatings on most packaging.

All dish cleaning should be done away from water sources. If you choose to use soap for cleaning, use biodegradable soap. While it is a common belief that biodegradable soap can safely be used in streams, lakes, and other water sources, that is not true. Even biodegradable soap can increase nitrogen levels and negatively impact aquatic life.

Before cleaning your dishes, remove any food scraps (a food scraper is especially helpful). The remaining waste water should be spread out over a wide area and away from water sources, never in them. Food scraps should be packed out, not buried, to prevent wildlife from learning to get food from areas where humans camp, and to prevent them from damaging an area to access buried food.

Base Recipes

BEEF MEATBALLS, ITALIAN-STYLE

Makes 8 servings

INGREDIENTS

1 pound ground beef

3/4 cup panko bread crumbs

1/4 cup grated parmesan cheese

1 egg, whisked

1 teaspoon oregano

1 teaspoon basil

1/2 teaspoon garlic powder

1 teaspoon kosher salt

1/8 teaspoon ground black pepper

DIRECTIONS

In a food processor, add all of the ingredients and pulse until combined.

Using an ice cream scoop or spoon, form into 24 meatballs.

Bake at 325 degrees for 20 minutes.

Let cool, cut each meatball into 8 pieces and place on dehydrator trays.

Dehydrate at 155 degrees until completely dry.

Store in the freezer until ready to use in recipes.

Use 3 meatballs (24 cut pieces) per recipe.

Nutrition info (per serving): calories 147; fat 8g; cholesterol 61mg; sodium 253mg; carbohydrates 6g; protein 14g

BISCUITS

Makes 24 biscuits (8 servings)

INGREDIENTS

2-2/3 cups all-purpose flour

3 tablespoons cornstarch

2 tablespoons whole egg powder

1/2 cup buttermilk powder

2 tablespoons butter powder

1 teaspoon baking soda

2 teaspoons baking powder

1/4 teaspoon garlic powder

1 /2 teaspoon oregano, dried

1/2 teaspoon rosemary, dried

1 teaspoon kosher salt

1-1/2 cups water

INGREDIENT NOTES

egg powder: purchase dried whole egg powder; dehydrating cooked eggs is not recommended

DIRECTIONS

Preheat the oven to 425 degrees and line a baking sheet with parchment paper or a baking mat.

In a large bowl, combine the flour, cornstarch, baking powder, baking soda, egg powder, garlic powder, herbs, and salt. Whisk together to combine well.

Make a well in the center of the flour mixture and add the water slowly. Use a fork to whisk the two together.

Stir until the biscuits just come together, taking care not to over mix.

Use an ice cream scoop or two large spoons to drop onto a baking sheet.

Bake the biscuits for 10-15 minutes until the tops are light golden brown.

Remove from the oven and cool.

Cut each biscuit into 8 pieces with a bread knife.

Spread on dehydrator sheets.

Dehydrate for 6-8 hours at 135 degrees until completely dry.

Store in an airtight container.

Nutrition info (3 biscuits): calories 193; fat 2g; cholesterol 35mg; sodium 365mg; carbohydrates 34g; protein 8g

CHICKEN MEATBALLS, ASIAN-STYLE

Makes 36 meatballs (12 servings)

INGREDIENTS

2 pounds ground chicken

1 cup onion, sliced

1 tablespoon ginger, chopped roughly

4 cloves garlic, peeled

1 cup Panko bread crumbs

1 teaspoon kosher salt

1/2 teaspoon ground black pepper

DIRECTIONS

In a food processor, add onions, ginger, and garlic and pulse to chop for a few seconds. Add chicken, panko bread crumbs, and salt. Pulse to combine.

Use an ice cream scoop or two spoons to form into 36 meatballs. Place on parchment-lined baking sheets.

Bake at 425 degrees for 20-25 minutes until lightly browned.

Cut each meatball into 8 pieces.

Dehydrate at 155 degrees until completely dry.

Store in the freezer until ready to use in recipes.

Nutrition info (per serving): calories 154; fat 8g; cholesterol 57mg; sodium 166mg; carbohydrates 7g; protein 14g

CHICKEN MEATBALLS, ITALIAN-STYLE

Makes 24 meatballs (8 servings)

INGREDIENTS

1 pound ground chicken

1 cup panko bread crumbs

1 egg, whisked

2 teaspoons Worcestershire sauce

1 teaspoon oregano

1 teaspoon sugar

1/2 teaspoon garlic powder

1 teaspoon kosher salt

1/8 teaspoon black pepper

DIRECTIONS

In a food processor, add all of the ingredients and pulse until combined.

Using an ice cream scoop or spoon, form into 24 meatballs.

Bake at 325 degrees for 20 minutes.

Let cool for 15 minutes.

Cut each meatball into 8 pieces and place on dehydrator trays.

Dehydrate at 155 degrees until completely dry.

Store in the freezer until ready to use in recipes.

Nutrition info (per serving): calories 134; fat 6g; cholesterol 66mg; sodium 227mg; carbohydrates 8g; protein 12g

PULLED PORK, MEXICAN-STYLE

Makes 12 servings

INGREDIENTS

For salsa verde:
1-1/2 pounds tomatillos, hulled and rinsed
1 jalapeno, sliced (optional)
1 bunch cilantro, chopped roughly
5-6 cloves garlic, peeled
1 tablespoon cumin powder
1/2 teaspoon kosher salt

For the pork:
2 pounds pork loin
salsa verde (recipe above)
2 large onions, sliced
2 teaspoons Mexican oregano
1 teaspoon smoked paprika
2 teaspoons cumin powder
1 teaspoon kosher salt

DIRECTIONS

Prepare salsa verde: Cover tomatillos in a 2-quart pan with water. Bring it to a boil and cook for 5-10 minutes. Drain all water except 1/2 cup. Pour into food processor, add remaining ingredients and 1/2 cup saved water. Blend to a smooth paste.

Pulled pork: Mix the spices and rub over the pork. In a slow cooker, spread onions in the base. Place the pork loin over the onions. Pour the salsa verde on top. Cook on high for 6 hours. When finished cooking, use two forks to pull apart and shred the pork. Cool. Spread the shredded pork with its sauce on dehydrating trays. Dehydrate at 155 degrees for 10 hours or more until completely dry. Place in a plastic bag or vacuum seal and store in the freezer until ready to use.

Nutrition info (per serving): calories 115; fat 3g; cholesterol 30mg; sodium 511mg; carbohydrates 7g; protein 6g

TOMATO CURRY BASE

Makes 16 servings

INGREDIENTS

4 cups onions, chopped
1 can (28-ounce) crushed tomatoes
1/2 non-fat Greek yogurt
8 cloves garlic, chopped
1 tablespoon ginger, chopped
2 teaspoons cumin seeds
1 bay leaf
4 green cardamom pods
2-1/2 teaspoons coriander powder
1/2 teaspoon chili powder
1 teaspoon turmeric powder
1/2 teaspoon kosher salt
1 tablespoon olive oil

DIRECTIONS

Heat oil in a 2-quart pan. Add bay leaf, cardamom, ginger, and garlic. Sauté for a few seconds till you can smell aroma.

Add onions, coriander powder, chili powder, and salt and cook until translucent.

Add tomatoes and cook for another 5-10 minutes.

Add yogurt and stir to combine.

Cook for 4-5 minutes.

Cool, spread on dehydrator trays and dehydrate at 125 degrees until completely dry.

Break the tomato bark into pieces and process it in a food processor to a powder.

Store in an airtight container.

Nutrition info (1 tablespoon): calories 44; fat 1g; cholesterol 0mg; sodium 44mg; carbohydrates 8g; protein 2g

Almond Berry Oatmeal

Oatmeal doesn't have to be boring! Make your own healthier version with whole rolled oats, almonds, dried berries, and the creaminess of coconut milk powder.

difficulty rating ★✰✰✰   recipe by Lisa   🌿 vegetarian

Nutrition info: calories 611; fat 32g; cholesterol 0mg; sodium 0mg; carbohydrates 70g; protein 11g

Makes 1 serving

INGREDIENTS

1/2 cup whole rolled oats

1 tablespoon organic cane sugar

2 tablespoons coconut milk powder

2 teaspoons chia seeds

2 tablespoons sliced almonds

2 tablespoons freeze-dried blueberries, strawberries, raspberries, or a mix of all three

1/4 teaspoon vanilla bean powder

1 tablespoon coconut oil

INGREDIENT NOTES

almonds: substitute with cashews, pecans or walnuts

coconut milk powder: whole milk powder can be used instead, but non-fat milk powder is not recommended

freeze-dried berries: any type of dried fruit can be used instead

whole rolled oats: instant oats can be used instead but may lead to a mushier texture

AT HOME

Mix all ingredients together and package in a plastic bag or vacuum seal.

Package coconut oil separately.

AT CAMP

Bring 1/2 cup (4 ounces) of water to a boil.

Add all ingredients and stir well.

Simmer on low for 1-2 minutes, stirring frequently.

Turn off heat, add coconut oil, cover and let sit for 5 minutes.

Reheat if needed.

Biscuits & Sausage Gravy

This hearty breakfast favorite tastes just like the made-from-scratch version – but can be easily made without fuss at camp and enjoyed in the backcountry.

difficulty rating ★★★☆   recipe by Sanjana

Nutrition info: calories 480; fat 18g; cholesterol 90mg; sodium 1,004mg; carbohydrates 51g; protein 22g

Makes 1 serving

INGREDIENTS

3 dehydrated biscuits, each cut into 8 pieces (see recipe on page 23)

1/4 cup freeze-dried sausage

4 teaspoons all-purpose flour

2 tablespoons whole milk powder

1 tablespoon butter powder

1 teaspoon nutritional yeast

1/4 teaspoon onion powder

1/8 teaspoon garlic powder

1/8 teaspoon thyme, dried

1/8 teaspoon oregano, dried

1/4 teaspoon kosher salt

1/8 teaspoon ground black pepper

INGREDIENT NOTES

nutritional yeast: used as a healthy substitute for chicken bouillon

whole milk powder: heavy cream powder can be used instead, but non-fat milk powder is not recommended

AT HOME

Toast the flour in a heavy pan for 5-7 minutes until you begin to smell it toasting, being careful to not burn the flour.

Remove from heat and allow to cool.

Mix all ingredients together and package in a plastic bag or vacuum seal.

AT CAMP

Bring 3/4 cup (6 ounces) of water to a boil.

Add all ingredients and stir well.

Simmer on low for 1-2 minutes, stirring frequently.

Turn off heat, cover and let soak for 15 minutes.

Reheat if needed.

Creamy Polenta

*This creamy and savory breakfast is loaded with the flavors
of sun-dried tomatoes, Parmesan cheese, and bacon jerky.
It's also easy to put together and quick to cook at camp.*

difficulty rating ★☆☆☆   *recipe by Sanjana*

Nutrition info: calories 397; fat 20g; cholesterol 134mg; sodium 510mg; carbohydrates 39g; protein 17g

Makes 1 serving

INGREDIENTS

1/3 cup instant polenta

1/2 ounce bacon jerky, chopped into pieces

1 tablespoon sun-dried tomatoes, chopped

2 tablespoons Parmesan cheese, shredded

1 tablespoon butter powder

1 tablespoon whole egg powder

1/4 teaspoon oregano, dried

1/4 teaspoon kosher salt

1/8 teaspoon ground black pepper

1 teaspoon olive oil

INGREDIENT NOTES

bacon jerky: use shelf stable bacon or bacon jerky – dehydrating bacon is not recommended

egg powder: purchase dried whole egg powder instead of dehydrating cooked eggs

instant polenta: finely ground cornmeal can be used instead

sun-dried tomatoes: purchase sun-dried tomatoes that are not packed in oil

AT HOME

Mix all ingredients (except olive oil and Parmesan cheese) together and package in a plastic bag or vacuum seal.

Package olive oil and Parmesan cheese separately.

AT CAMP

Bring 3/4 cup (6 ounces) of water to a boil.

Add package of dried ingredients, cheese and olive oil. Stir well to mix.

Turn off heat, cover and let soak for 10 minutes.

Egg Scramble

Powdered eggs are a game-changer for cooking eggs in the backcountry. This version of scrambled eggs packs a lot of flavor with shredded potatoes, bacon jerky, cheddar cheese, peppers, and onions.

difficulty rating ★★☆☆   *recipe by Sanjana*

Nutrition info: calories 406; fat 23g; cholesterol 393mg; sodium 718mg; carbohydrates 17g; protein 22g

Makes 1 serving

INGREDIENTS

1/4 cup whole egg powder

1/4 cup shredded potatoes, dehydrated

1/2 ounce bacon jerky, chopped

1 tablespoon shredded cheddar cheese, freeze dried

1 teaspoon green onions, dehydrated

1 tablespoon mushrooms, dehydrated

1-1/2 teaspoons roasted peppers, dehydrated

1-1/2 teaspoons onions, dehydrated

1 tablespoon butter powder

1/8 teaspoon kosher salt

1/8 teaspoon ground black pepper

INGREDIENT NOTES

bacon jerky: use shelf stable bacon or bacon jerky – dehydrating bacon is not recommended

cheese, freeze-dried: substitute with 1 teaspoon cheddar cheese powder

egg powder: purchase dried whole egg powder instead of dehydrating cooked eggs

green onions: slice green onions (white and green parts) and dehydrate

roasted peppers: chop canned or frozen roasted peppers into small pieces and dehydrate

shredded potatoes: cook whole potatoes, then shred and dehydrate

AT HOME

Mix all ingredients together and package in a plastic bag or vacuum seal.

Package bacon jerky separately.

AT CAMP

Bring 3/4 cup (6 ounces) of water to a boil.

Add all ingredients. Simmer on low heat and stir constantly until egg comes together, being careful to not burn.

Turn off heat, cover and let sit for 10 minutes.

Ginger Peach Cashew Oatmeal

Update your morning oats, making them healthier and tastier with dried peaches, cashews, ginger, and the creaminess of coconut milk powder. Chia seeds provide energy boosting benefits.

difficulty rating ★☆☆☆   *recipe by Lisa*   🌿 *vegetarian*

Nutrition info: calories 619; fat 38g; cholesterol 0mg; sodium 0mg; carbohydrates 59g; protein 12g

Makes 1 serving

INGREDIENTS

1/2 cup whole rolled oats

1 tablespoon organic cane sugar

2 tablespoons coconut milk powder

2 teaspoons chia seeds

2 tablespoons chopped dried peaches

2 tablespoons chopped roasted cashews

1/2 teaspoon ground ginger

1 tablespoon coconut oil

INGREDIENT NOTES

cashews: substitute with almonds, pecans or walnuts

coconut milk powder: whole milk powder can be used instead, but non-fat milk powder is not recommended

peaches: substitute dried apples, nectarines or apricots

whole rolled oats: instant oats can be used instead but may lead to a mushier texture

AT HOME

Mix all ingredients together and package in a plastic bag or vacuum seal.

Package coconut oil separately.

AT CAMP

Bring 1/2 cup (4 ounces) of water to a boil.

Add all ingredients and stir well.

Simmer on low for 1-2 minutes, stirring frequently.

Turn off heat, add coconut oil, cover and let sit for 5 minutes.

Reheat if needed.

Hash Browns

This hearty breakfast meal combines dehydrated shredded potatoes with black beans and roasted red peppers in a light cheese sauce.

difficulty rating ★★☆☆   *recipe by Lisa*   🌿 *vegetarian*

Nutrition info: calories 481; fat 17g; cholesterol 9mg; sodium 434mg; carbohydrates 46g; protein 11g

Makes 1 serving

INGREDIENTS

2 ounces shredded potatoes, dehydrated

1/4 cup black beans, dehydrated

1 tablespoon green onions, dehydrated

1 tablespoon roasted red pepper, dehydrated

1 tablespoon Parmesan cheese powder

1 teaspoon butter powder

1/4 teaspoon poultry seasoning

1/4 teaspoon kosher salt

1/8 teaspoon ground black pepper

1 tablespoon olive oil

INGREDIENT NOTES

black beans: dehydrate fully cooked beans

green onions: slice green onions (white and green parts) and dehydrate

poultry seasoning: substitute with a mix of sage, thyme and rosemary

roasted red pepper: dehydrated canned roasted red peppers or substitute purchased freeze-dried peppers

shredded potatoes: cook whole potatoes, then shred and dehydrate

AT HOME

Mix all ingredients except Parmesan cheese together and package in a plastic bag or vacuum seal. Package Parmesan cheese separately.

AT CAMP

Bring 1 cup (8 ounces) of water to a full boil.

Add ingredients and stir well.

Turn off heat, cover and let sit for 10 minutes until fully rehydrated.

Add olive oil and Parmesan cheese.

Reheat if needed.

Chocolate Chip Peanut Butter Bars

*These soft energy bars are full of nutty flavor
and have plenty of protein to support physical activity.*

difficulty rating ★★☆☆   *recipe by Lisa*   🍃 *vegetarian*

Nutrition info: calories 438; fat 26g; cholesterol 0mg; sodium 108mg; carbohydrates 44g; protein 10g

Makes 8 bars

INGREDIENTS

2 cups whole rolled oats

1/2 cup chocolate chips

1/2 cup peanuts, chopped

3 tablespoons almond protein powder

1 tablespoon flax seeds

1/2 teaspoon vanilla powder

1/4 teaspoon salt

1/2 cup peanut butter

1/3 cup brown rice syrup

1/2 cup oat milk

1/4 cup coconut oil

INGREDIENT NOTES

almond protein powder: any type of protein powder can be substituted

brown rice syrup: substitute with light corn syrup

chocolate chips: substitute with white chocolate chips, peanut butter chips, or butterscotch chips

oats: whole rolled oats are preferred over instant oats for the thicker texture

peanut butter: use any type of nut butter

vanilla powder: to vary the flavor, substitute cinnamon or ginger powder

DIRECTIONS

Preheat oven to 350 degrees.

Use a food processor to chop the oats into a mix of smaller pieces. Roughly chop the peanuts.

In a large mixing bowl, combine oats, protein powder, chocolate chips, peanuts, flax seeds, vanilla powder and salt. Set aside.

In a small pan, combine the peanut butter, brown rice syrup, oat milk, and coconut oil. Heat just until the coconut oil liquifies. Let cool completely before adding to the dry mixture.

Add the liquid ingredients to the dry mixture and stir well until all ingredients are fully incorporated.

Use either a silicone bar baking dish or a glass 8"x8" baking pan coated lightly with cooking spray.

Spread mixture evenly, pressing down firmly with a spatula or your hands (place plastic wrap over the mixture first) until evenly distributed.

Bake for 30 minutes until edges are lightly browned.

Remove from oven and let cool completely before removing from the silicone bar baking dish or before cutting into bars.

Store bars in the freezer until ready to use.

Ginger Mango Rice Crispy Bars

Loaded with the flavors of ginger and mango, these rice crispy bars are a crunchy alternative to boring trail bars.

difficulty rating ★★☆☆　*recipe by Lisa*　🌿 *vegetarian*

Nutrition info: calories 180; fat 11g; cholesterol 0mg; sodium 53mg; carbohydrates 17g; protein 5g

Makes 8 bars

INGREDIENTS

1/2 cup almonds

1/2 cup cashews

1/3 cup sesame seeds

2/3 cup crisp brown rice cereal

1/4 cup chopped dried mango, finely chopped

1/4 cup candied ginger, finely chopped

1/4 cup brown rice syrup

1/8 teaspoon fine sea salt

1/2 teaspoon ground ginger

1/8 teaspoon ground cardamom

INGREDIENT NOTES

almonds, cashews: roasted and salted nuts are preferred; any type of nuts can be substituted in equal amounts

brown rice cereal: use regular rice crispy cereal if you can't find brown rice puffs

brown rice syrup: substitute with light corn syrup

mango: any type of dried fruit can be used

DIRECTIONS

Preheat oven to 325 degrees.

Finely chop almonds and cashews using a food processor. The mixture should be part crumbs, part small pieces of nuts.

Add the chopped nuts, mango, sesame seeds, brown rice cereal, salt, ginger, and cardamom to a large bowl and stir until thoroughly mixed.

Pour the syrup over the mixture and incorporate until the dry ingredients are evenly coated with the syrup.

In a silicone bar pan (or a glass 8"x8" baking pan coated lightly with cooking spray), spread the mixture evenly, pressing down firmly with a spatula or your hands (place plastic wrap over the mixture first) until compacted and evenly distributed in the pan.

Bake in the preheated oven for 20 minutes, or until slightly browned at the edges.

Remove from oven and let cool completely before removing from the baking pan.

If using a baking dish, cut into 8 bars.

Store bars in the freezer until ready to use.

Lemongrass Curry Trail Mix

A spicy twist on traditional trail mix, this version combines nuts and seeds with dried cherries, mango, and coconut and is coated with a curry spice mix.

difficulty rating ★★★☆   *recipe by Sanjana*   🌿 *vegetarian*

Nutrition info: calories 156; fat 10g; cholesterol 0mg; sodium 130mg; carbohydrates 13g; protein 5g

Makes 24 servings (1/4 cup each)

INGREDIENTS

1-1/2 cups whole rolled oats

1/2 cup roasted peanuts

1/2 cup raw cashews

1/2 cup raw almonds

1/4 cup pistachios

1/4 cup pumpkin seeds

1/4 cup sunflower seeds

1/4 cup coconut chips

1/2 cup tart dried cherries

1 tablespoon white sesame seeds

1/2 cup chopped dried mango

Spices

6-7 kaffir lime leaves – dried or fresh, chiffonade

2 tablespoons lemongrass paste

1 tablespoon fresh lime juice

1 tablespoon brown sugar

1-1/2 teaspoons kosher salt

1 teaspoon liquid aminos or soy sauce

1/4 cup coconut oil

1 teaspoon (2 packets) crystallized lime powder

1/2 teaspoon red curry paste powder, dehydrated (see ingredient notes on page 101)

1/4 teaspoon turmeric powder

DIRECTIONS

Preheat oven to 275 degrees.

Mix oats, nuts, seeds and fruit in a bowl.

Heat oil in a pan. Add lemongrass paste and cook on low heat for one minute, stirring continuously. Add Kaffir lime leaves and remove from heat.

Add lime juice and spices (except crystallized lime powder).

Add the lemongrass mixture to the nuts and oats mixture and mix well to incorporate.

Line a baking sheet with parchment paper and spread the combined mixture evenly.

Place baking sheet on the center shelf. Bake for 30 minutes.

Add crystallized lime powder and mix well.

Turn off the oven and place the baking sheet in the oven with the door open to allow to cool.

Let cool completely before serving.

Sesame Oat Bars

*Making your own protein bars is economical, and easy if
you use a silicone bar pan! These bars contain peanut butter
combined with whole oats and sesame seeds.*

difficulty rating ★★☆☆   *recipe by Lisa*   🌿 *vegetarian*

Nutrition info: calories 303; fat 14g; cholesterol 0mg; sodium 195mg; carbohydrates 38g; protein 6g

Makes 8 bars

INGREDIENTS

2 1/4 cups organic rolled oats

1/2 cup brown rice syrup

1/4 cup coconut oil

1/4 cup creamy peanut butter

2 tablespoons sesame seeds

1/2 teaspoon salt

INGREDIENT NOTES

brown rice syrup: substitute with light corn syrup

oats: whole oats will provide a better texture than instant or quick cooking oats

peanut butter: use any type of nut butter

DIRECTIONS

Preheat oven to 360 degrees.

Place the oats in a food processor and pulse until the oats are cut into small pieces.

Toast the sesame seeds in a small skillet until very lightly browned.

Mix the oats, sesame seeds and salt in a mixing bowl.

Heat the coconut oil just enough to liquify it. Add the brown rice syrup and peanut butter. Blend well.

Pour the liquid mixture into the oat mixture and stir to combine. Use your hands to fully incorporate the ingredients (wet your hands first to prevent excessive sticking).

Use either a silicone bar baking dish or a glass 8"x8" baking pan coated lightly with cooking spray.

Spread mixture evenly, pressing down firmly with a spatula or your hands (place plastic wrap over the mixture first) until evenly distributed.

Bake in the preheated oven for 20 minutes or until slightly browned at the edges.

Cool for about 20 minutes then release the bars from the pan.

Store in the freezer until ready to use.

Asian Noodle Salad

Sweet, salty and nutty – this refreshing cold soak noodle salad includes red peppers, pineapple, zucchini, and cashews in a sesame-soy-ginger sauce.

difficulty rating ★★☆☆   *recipe by Lisa*   🌿 *vegetarian*

Nutrition info: calories 418; fat 14g; cholesterol 0mg; sodium 697mg; carbohydrates 65g; protein 13g

Makes 1 serving

INGREDIENTS

1-1/2 ounces angel hair pasta, dehydrated

2 tablespoons zucchini, dehydrated

1 tablespoon pineapple, dehydrated

1 tablespoon red peppers, dehydrated

2 teaspoons green onions, dehydrated

2 tablespoons cashews, roughly chopped

1/4 teaspoon garlic powder

1/8 teaspoon onion powder

1/2 teaspoon ground ginger

1 teaspoon sesame seeds

2 teaspoons soy sauce

2 teaspoons sesame oil

INGREDIENT NOTES

angel hair pasta: break into small pieces and pre-cook, then rinse and dehydrate

cashews: use roasted salted cashews for best flavor; or replace with salted peanuts

green onions: slice green onions (white and green parts) and dehydrate

pineapple: dehydrate canned crushed pineapple

red peppers: chop canned or frozen roasted peppers into small pieces and dehydrate

zucchini: slice into quarters and dehydrate

AT HOME

Mix all ingredients together and package in a plastic bag or vacuum seal.

Package soy sauce and sesame oil in a separate container.

AT CAMP

Add dry ingredients to a jar or cup with a lid.

Add 1/2 cup (4 ounces) of cold water, soy sauce and sesame oil. Stir well.

Press on the top of the ingredients so they are sitting in the liquid.

Cover and soak for at 10 minutes. Stir to reincorporate ingredients into the liquid. Soak for another 10 minutes until all ingredients are fully rehydrated.

Burrito Bowl

*This cold soak lunch pairs black beans and rice with pulled pork,
fire-roasted corn, and peppers for a spicy, hearty meal.*

difficulty rating ★★★☆   *recipe by Sanjana*

Nutrition info: calories 400; fat 16g; cholesterol 15mg; sodium 673mg; carbohydrates 46g; protein 18g

Makes 1 serving

INGREDIENTS

1/4 cup pulled pork, dehydrated (see recipe on page 25)

1/2 cup basmati rice, dehydrated

1/4 cup black beans, dehydrated

2 tablespoons fire-roasted peppers and onions, dehydrated

1 tablespoon fire-roasted corn, dehydrated

1 tablespoon mild roasted Hatch chilies, dehydrated

1/2 teaspoon taco seasoning

1/4 teaspoon Mexican oregano, dried

1/4 teaspoon cumin powder

1 teaspoon cilantro, dried

1/4 teaspoon kosher salt

1/2 teaspoon (1 packet) crystallized lime powder

1 tablespoon olive oil

1 flour tortilla (optional)

INGREDIENT NOTES

black beans: dehydrate canned or fully cooked black beans

crystallized lime powder: substitute with 1 teaspoon fresh lime juice (packaged separately)

fire-roasted corn: dehydrate canned or frozen corn

fire-roasted peppers and onions: substitute with dehydrated fresh or frozen bell peppers and onions

Hatch chilies: substitute with canned green mild peppers

vegetarian option: use an additional 1/4 cup dehydrated black beans instead of the pulled pork

AT HOME

Mix all ingredients together and package in a plastic bag or vacuum seal.

Package olive oil separately.

AT CAMP

Add all ingredients to a jar or cup with a lid.

Add 3/4 cup (6 ounces) of cold water and olive oil and stir well.

Press on the top of the ingredients so they are sitting in the liquid.

Cover and soak for at least 30 minutes until all ingredients are fully rehydrated.

Optional: Wrap in a flour tortilla for a burrito.

Greek Orzo Salad

This cold soak lemony salad combines orzo with peppers, onions, tomatoes, olives, and chickpeas for a fresh-tasting meal on trail.

difficulty rating ★★☆☆   *recipe by Lisa* 🌿 *vegetarian*

Nutrition info: calories 474; fat 21g; cholesterol 0mg; sodium 775mg; carbohydrates 66g; protein 15g

Makes 1 serving

INGREDIENTS

1/2 cup orzo, dehydrated

1/4 cup fire-roasted peppers and onions, dehydrated

1/4 cup tomatoes, dehydrated

2 tablespoons chickpeas, dehydrated

1 tablespoon black olives, dehydrated

1/2 teaspoon (1 packet) crystallized lemon powder

1/2 teaspoon Greek oregano

1/4 teaspoon salt

1 tablespoon olive oil

INGREDIENT NOTES

black olives: slice canned olives and dehydrate

chickpeas: dehydrate canned or fully cooked chickpeas

crystallized lemon powder: substitute with 1 teaspoon fresh lemon juice (packaged separately)

fire-roasted peppers and onions: substitute with dehydrated fresh or frozen bell peppers and onions

orzo: pre-cook, rinse and dehydrate

tomatoes: sun-dried tomatoes can be used instead of dehydrated tomatoes

AT HOME

Mix all ingredients together and package in a plastic bag or vacuum seal.

Package olive oil separately.

AT CAMP

Add all ingredients to a jar or cup with a lid.

Add 1 cup (8 ounces) of cold water and olive oil and stir well.

Press on the top of the ingredients so they are sitting in the liquid.

Cover and soak for at least 2 hours until all ingredients are fully rehydrated.

Kale & Lentil Salad

*A cold soak kale and lentil salad with the fresh flavors
of lime and mint make for a refreshing lunch.*

difficulty rating ★★★☆   *recipe by Sanjana*   🌿 *vegetarian*

Nutrition info: calories 371; fat 24g; cholesterol 0mg; sodium 440mg; carbohydrates 27g; protein 12g

Makes 1 serving

INGREDIENTS

*1/3 cup lentils, dehydrated
(see recipe in right column)*

1 tablespoon shredded carrot, dehydrated

1 tablespoon green onion, dehydrated

1 tablespoon green olives, dehydrated

1 tablespoon cashews, chopped

1/8 teaspoon garlic powder

1/4 teaspoon toasted cumin seeds

1/8 teaspoon red chili pepper (optional)

*1/2 teaspoon (1 packet) crystallized lime
powder*

1/4 teaspoon mint, dried

1/4 teaspoon kosher salt

1 tablespoon olive oil

INGREDIENT NOTES

carrots: shred fresh carrots and dehydrate

cashews: roasted nuts provide the best
flavor; substitute with any type of nut

cumin seeds: toast cumin seeds in a skillet
until slight browned

crystallized lime powder: substitute with
1 teaspoon fresh lime juice (packaged
separately)

green olives: slice thin and dehydrate;
kalamata or black olives also work well in this
recipe

green onions: slice green onions (white and
green parts) and dehydrate

mint: dehydrate fresh mint for the best flavor

PREPARING THE LENTILS

Makes 6 servings

INGREDIENTS

*1 cup dried red whole lentils,
soaked for 4 hours, and drained*

1 teaspoon turmeric powder

1 teaspoon kosher salt

DIRECTIONS

In a 4-quart pan, bring 2 cups of water to a
boil. Add drained lentils, turmeric, and salt.
Reduce heat to simmer. Cook uncovered for
25-30 minutes.

Once cooked, drain and let cool. Spread
on dehydrator trays and dehydrate at 135
degrees until completely dry.

AT HOME

Mix all ingredients together and package in a
plastic bag or vacuum seal. Package olive oil
separately.

AT CAMP

Add all ingredients to a jar or cup with a lid.

Add 3/4 cup (6 ounces) of cold water and olive oil
and stir well. Press on the top of the ingredients so
they are sitting in the liquid.

Cover and soak for at least 20 minutes until fully
rehydrated.

Smoky Bean Power Salad

This cold soak salad combines four beans with a hint of lemon and veggies to create a sweet and smoky protein powerhouse.

difficulty rating ★★★☆   *recipe by Sanjana*   🌿 *vegetarian*

Nutrition info: calories 522; fat 17g; cholesterol 0mg; sodium 324mg; carbohydrates 69g; protein 21g

Makes 1 serving

INGREDIENTS

1/4 cup black beans, dehydrated

1/4 cup kidney beans, dehydrated

1/4 cup chickpeas, dehydrated

1 tablespoon green beans, dehydrated

1 tablespoon roasted corn, dehydrated

1-1/2 teaspoons fire-roasted peppers and onions, dehydrated

1 tablespoon green onions, dehydrated

1/4 teaspoon chipotle powder

1/4 teaspoon cumin powder

1/8 teaspoon garlic powder

1/4 teaspoon Mexican oregano

1/4 teaspoon brown sugar

1 teaspoon (2 packets) crystallized lemon powder

1/4 teaspoon salt

1 tablespoon olive oil

INGREDIENT NOTES

black beans: dehydrate canned or fully cooked black beans

chickpeas: dehydrate canned or fully cooked chickpeas

chipotle powder: for a less spicy version, use smoked paprika

corn: dehydrate canned or frozen corn

crystallized lemon powder: substitute with 2 teaspoons fresh lemon juice (packaged separately)

fire-roasted peppers and onions: substitute with dehydrated fresh or frozen bell peppers and onions

green beans: dehydrate canned or frozen French-style green beans

green onions: slice green onions (white and green parts) and dehydrate

kidney beans: dehydrate canned or fully cooked kidney beans

AT HOME

Mix all ingredients together and package in a plastic bag or vacuum seal. Package olive oil separately.

AT CAMP

Add all ingredients to a jar or cup with a lid.

Add 3/4 cup (6 ounces) of cold water and olive oil and stir well.

Press on the top of the ingredients so they are sitting in the liquid.

Cover and soak for at least 30 minutes until all ingredients are rehydrated.

Zesty Thai Salad

This zesty rice salad is made with dehydrated cabbage, edamame, green onions, carrots, and peanuts – and has a spicy kick from red curry paste and lime powder.

difficulty rating ★★★☆   recipe by Sanjana

Nutrition info: calories 412; fat 24g; cholesterol 0mg; sodium 129mg; carbohydrates 22g; protein 20g

Makes 1 serving

INGREDIENTS

1/4 cup basmati rice, dehydrated

1/4 cup tofu, dehydrated

1/2 cup cabbage, dehydrated

1 tablespoon edamame, dehydrated

1 tablespoon green onions, sliced, dehydrated

1 tablespoon carrots, shredded, dehydrated

1/2 teaspoon red curry paste, dehydrated

1/2 teaspoon (1 packet) crystallized lime powder

2 tablespoons roasted peanuts

1/8 teaspoon Red Boat salt

2 teaspoons sesame oil

INGREDIENT NOTES

cabbage: shred fresh cabbage and dehydrate

carrots: shred fresh carrots and dehydrate

crystallized lime powder: substitute with 1 teaspoon fresh lime juice (packaged separately)

edamame: dehydrate frozen pre-shelled edamame

Red Boat salt: substitute with 1/2 teaspoon soy sauce (packaged separately)

red curry paste: use any prepared Thai curry paste without oil (Ma Ploy is a recommended brand) and dehydrate, then pulse in a food processor to make a powder; or substitute with red curry powder

tofu: freeze extra firm tofu, then defrost and cut into 1/2-inch cubes and dehydrate at 125 degrees for 8-10 hours

AT HOME

Mix all ingredients together and package in a plastic bag or vacuum seal.

Package sesame oil separately.

AT CAMP

Add all ingredients to a jar or cup with a lid.

Add 3/4 cups (6 ounces) of cold water and sesame oil (plus soy sauce if using instead of salt) and stir well.

Press on the top of the ingredients so they are sitting in the liquid.

Cover and soak for at least 30 minutes until all ingredients are fully rehydrated.

Artichoke-Spinach Alfredo Orzo

What's not to love about an alfredo pasta dish with spinach and artichokes? Add bacon jerky and mmm...

difficulty rating ★★☆☆   recipe by Lisa

Nutrition info: calories 444; fat 16g; cholesterol 51mg; sodium 565mg; carbohydrates 55g; protein 22g

Makes 1 serving

INGREDIENTS

2 ounces (1/2 cup) orzo, dehydrated

1/4 cup spinach, dehydrated

1/4 cup artichoke hearts, dehydrated

1 tablespoon butter powder

1 tablespoon heavy cream powder

1 tablespoon Parmesan cheese powder

1/4 teaspoon basil, dried

1/8 teaspoon ground black pepper

1/2 ounce bacon jerky

INGREDIENT NOTES

artichoke hearts: purchase canned artichoke hearts, cut into small pieces and dehydrate

bacon jerky: use shelf stable bacon or bacon jerky – dehydrating bacon is not recommended

heavy cream powder: whole milk powder can be used in this recipe, but we don't recommend using non-fat or skim milk powder

orzo: for better rehydrating, pre-cook and dehydrate or use a pasta that cooks in 5 minutes or less

spinach: chop fresh or frozen spinach and dehydrate

vegetarian option: instead of bacon, use 1/4 cup mushrooms and add 1/4 teaspoon salt

AT HOME

Add all ingredients except bacon jerky to a plastic bag or vacuum seal.

Package bacon jerky separately.

AT CAMP

Heat bacon in pan until hot. Remove and set aside.

Bring 1-1/4 cups (10 ounces) of water to a boil.

Add all ingredients and stir well.

Simmer for 1-2 minutes.

Turn off heat, cover and let sit for 15 minutes until all ingredients are fully rehydrated. Add bacon and reheat if needed.

If there's too much liquid, simmer uncovered for a few minutes, stirring constantly to prevent burning on the bottom of the pot.

Butternut Squash Risotto

Creamy risotto that's been pre-cooked and dehydrated is combined with winter squash and mushrooms.

difficulty rating ★★☆☆   *recipe by Lisa*   🌿 *vegetarian*

Nutrition info: calories 462; fat 20g; cholesterol 15mg; sodium 600mg; carbohydrates 66g; protein 8g

Makes 1 serving

INGREDIENTS

1/2 cup risotto, dehydrated

1/4 cup butternut squash, dehydrated

1/4 cup mushrooms, dehydrated

1 tablespoon green onions, dehydrated

1 tablespoon heavy cream powder

1 teaspoon nutritional yeast

1/2 teaspoon thyme, dried

1/4 teaspoon onion powder

1 teaspoon cornstarch

1/4 teaspoon kosher salt

1/8 teaspoon ground black pepper

1 tablespoon olive oil

INGREDIENT NOTES

butternut squash: any type of winter squash can be used; fully cook and cut into small cubes for dehydrating

green onions: slice green onions (white and green parts) and dehydrate

heavy cream powder: whole milk powder can be used instead, but we don't recommend using non-fat or skim milk powder

mushrooms: slice white button mushrooms or porcini mushrooms and dehydrate

nutritional yeast: used as a healthy substitute for chicken bouillon

risotto: pre-cook arborio rice in water or stock and dehydrate

DINNER

AT HOME

Mix all ingredients together and package in a plastic bag or vacuum seal.

Package olive oil separately.

AT CAMP

Bring 1 cup (8 ounces) of water to a full boil.

Add all of the ingredients (except olive oil) and stir well.

Turn the heat to low and simmer for 2 minutes.

Turn off the heat, cover and let sit for 20 minutes until all ingredients are fully rehydrated.

Add olive oil and reheat if needed.

If there's too much liquid, simmer uncovered for a few minutes, stirring constantly to prevent burning on the bottom of the pot.

Channa Masala

*Curried chickpeas with rice and spinach will tantalize
your taste buds with a wonderful combination of spices.*

difficulty rating ★★★☆   *recipe by Sanjana*   🌿 *vegetarian*

Nutrition info: calories 673; fat 23g; cholesterol 0mg; sodium 405mg; carbohydrates 98g; protein 25g

Makes 1 serving

INGREDIENTS

2 tablespoons tomato curry base, dehydrated
(see recipe on page 25)

1/2 cup chickpeas, dehydrated

1/2 cup basmati rice, dehydrated

2 tablespoons spinach, dehydrated

1/2 teaspoon (1 packet) crystallized lime
powder

1/2 teaspoon garam masala

1/2 teaspoon cumin powder

1 teaspoon cilantro, dehydrated

1 tablespoon (1 packet) ghee

1/4 teaspoon kosher salt

INGREDIENT NOTES

basmati rice: pre-cook and dehydrate; substitute
with long grain rice if needed

chickpeas: dehydrate canned or fully cooked
chickpeas

cilantro: dehydrate fresh cilantro or use dried

crystallized lime powder: substitute with 1
teaspoon fresh lime juice (packaged separately)

ghee: substitute with 1 tablespoon olive oil

spinach: chop fresh or frozen spinach and
dehydrate

AT HOME

Mix all ingredients together and
package in a plastic bag or vacuum
seal.

Package ghee separately.

AT CAMP

Bring 1-1/2 cups (12 ounces) of
water to a boil.

Add dried ingredients and ghee,
stir well to mix.

Simmer on low heat for 2 minutes.

Turn off heat, cover and let sit for
20 minutes until fully rehydrated.

Reheat if needed.

DINNER

Cheesy Broccoli Risotto

*Creamy risotto with broccoli and mushrooms
in a cheesy garlic thyme sauce.*

difficulty rating ★★☆☆   *recipe by Lisa*   🌿 *vegetarian*

Nutrition info: calories 422; fat 14g; cholesterol 44mg; sodium 682mg; carbohydrates 60g; protein 21g

Makes 1 serving

INGREDIENTS

1/2 cup risotto, dehydrated

1/2 cup broccoli, dehydrated or freeze-dried

1/3 cup mushrooms, dehydrated

1 tablespoon heavy cream powder

1 tablespoon butter powder

2 tablespoons Parmesan cheese powder

1/4 teaspoon garlic powder

1/2 teaspoon thyme, dried

1 teaspoon cornstarch

1/4 teaspoon kosher salt

1/8 teaspoon ground black pepper

INGREDIENT NOTES

broccoli: dehydrate pre-cooked or frozen broccoli

heavy cream powder: whole milk powder can be used instead, but we don't recommend using non-fat or skim milk powder

mushrooms: break dried mushrooms into small pieces

risotto: pre-cook arborio rice in water or stock and dehydrate

Parmesan cheese powder: add at the end of cooking to prevent sticking to the pan

AT HOME

Mix all ingredients together and package in a plastic bag or vacuum seal.

Package Parmesan cheese powder separately.

AT CAMP

Bring 1-1/2 cups (12 ounces) of water to a full boil.

Add dried ingredients and stir well.

Simmer on low heat for 2 minutes.

Turn off heat, cover and let sit for 15 minutes until fully rehydrated.

Add Parmesan cheese powder and stir to incorporate. Reheat if needed.

Chicken Curry

*This creamy curry dish with chicken meatballs and potatoes
is satisfying and flavorful without being too spicy.*

difficulty rating ★★★★   *recipe by Sanjana*

Nutrition info: calories 694; fat 34g; cholesterol 87mg; sodium 486mg; carbohydrates 76g; protein 24g

Makes 1 serving

INGREDIENTS

1/2 cup Asian-style chicken meatballs, dehydrated (see recipe on page 24)

3 tablespoons tomato curry base (see recipe on page 25)

1/2 cup basmati rice, dehydrated

1/4 cup cubed potatoes, dehydrated

2 tablespoons heavy cream powder

1/2 teaspoon brown sugar

1 teaspoon cilantro, dried

1 tablespoon (1 packet) ghee

1/8 teaspoon salt

INGREDIENT NOTES

basmati rice: pre-cook and dehydrate; substitute with long grain rice if needed

chicken meatballs: substitute with freeze-dried chicken or dehydrate canned chicken

ghee: substitute with 1 tablespoon olive oil

heavy cream powder: whole milk powder can be used instead, but we don't recommend using non-fat or skim milk powder

potatoes: cut into small cubes and boil until almost done, then dehydrate

AT HOME

Mix all ingredients together and package in a plastic bag or vacuum seal.

Package ghee separately.

AT CAMP

Bring 1-1/2 cups (12 ounces) of water to a boil.

Add dried ingredients and ghee. Stir well to mix.

Simmer on low heat for 2 minutes.

Turn off heat, cover and let sit for 20 minutes until fully rehydrated.

Reheat if needed.

DINNER

Chicken & Dumplings

A hearty comfort food, this meal combines chicken meatballs and biscuit pieces in a creamy sauce with peas and carrots.

difficulty rating ★★★★   *recipe by Sanjana*

Nutrition info: calories 582; fat 24g; cholesterol 135mg; sodium 672mg; carbohydrates 64g; protein 31g

Makes 1 serving

INGREDIENTS

1/4 cup Asian-style chicken meatballs, dehydrated (see recipe on page 24)

3 dehydrated biscuits, each cut into 8 pieces (see recipe on page 23)

1-1/2 tablespoons carrots, dehydrated

1 tablespoon petite peas, dehydrated

3 tablespoons instant potato flakes

1 tablespoon butter powder

1 tablespoon heavy cream powder

2 tablespoons whole milk powder

2 teaspoons nutritional yeast

1/4 teaspoon onion powder

INGREDIENT NOTES

carrots: dice carrots, boil for 10 minutes, drain and dehydrate (or use frozen carrot pieces)

chicken meatballs: substitute with freeze-dried chicken, or dehydrate canned chicken

heavy cream powder: whole milk powder can be used in this recipe, but we don't recommend using non-fat or skim milk powder

instant potato flakes: we recommend brands without additives, such as Bob's Red Mill

nutritional yeast: used as a healthy substitute for chicken bouillon

peas: dehydrate frozen petite peas

AT HOME

Mix all ingredients together and package in a plastic bag or vacuum seal.

AT CAMP

Bring 1 cup (8 ounces) of water to a full boil.

Add dried ingredients and stir well.

Simmer on low heat for 2 minutes.

Turn off heat, cover and let sit for 15 minutes until fully rehydrated.

Add olive oil and reheat if needed.

If there's too much liquid, simmer uncovered for a few minutes, stirring constantly to prevent burning on the bottom of the pot.

Chicken & Noodles

A spin on classic chicken noodle casserole, this version uses chicken meatballs with egg noodles and roasted red peppers in a parsley, sage, and thyme sauce.

difficulty rating ★★★☆   recipe by Lisa

Nutrition info: calories 596; fat 27g; cholesterol 125mg; sodium 604mg; carbohydrates 64g; protein 26g

Makes 1 serving

INGREDIENTS

2 ounces wide egg noodles, dehydrated

1/4 cup Italian-style chicken meatballs, dehydrated (see recipe on page 24)

1 tablespoon roasted red pepper, dehydrated

1/4 cup mushrooms, dehydrated

1 tablespoon green onions, dehydrated

1 tablespoon butter powder

1 teaspoon cornstarch

1 tablespoon nutritional yeast

1/4 teaspoon onion powder

1/4 teaspoon parsley

1/8 teaspoon garlic powder

1/8 teaspoon thyme

1/8 teaspoon oregano

1/2 teaspoon poultry seasoning

1/4 teaspoon kosher salt

1/8 teaspoon ground black pepper

1 tablespoon olive oil

INGREDIENT NOTES

chicken meatballs: substitute with freeze-dried chicken, or dehydrate canned chicken

egg noodles: pre-cook and dehydrate or use noodles that cook in 5 minutes or less

green onions: slice green onions (white and green parts) and dehydrate

mushrooms: slice white button mushrooms or porcini mushrooms and dehydrate

nutritional yeast: used as a healthy substitute for chicken bouillon

poultry seasoning: substitute with a mix of sage, thyme and rosemary

roasted red pepper: dehydrate fresh, canned or frozen red peppers

AT HOME

Mix all ingredients together and package in a plastic bag or vacuum seal. Package olive oil separately.

AT CAMP

Bring 1 cup (8 ounces) of water to a full boil.

Add dried ingredients and stir well. Simmer on low heat for 2 minutes.

Turn off heat, cover and let sit for 15 minutes until fully rehydrated. Add olive oil and reheat if needed.

DINNER

Chicken Piccata

*Homemade chicken meatballs are combined with a hearty
pasta, capers, and mushrooms in a buttery lemon garlic sauce.*

difficulty rating ★★★☆   *recipe by Lisa*

Nutrition info: calories 535; fat 25g; cholesterol 80mg; sodium 690mg; carbohydrates 62g; protein 22g

Makes 1 serving

INGREDIENTS

2 ounces pasta, dehydrated

1/4 cup Italian-style chicken meatballs, dehydrated (see recipe on page 24)

2 teaspoons capers, dehydrated

1/4 cup mushrooms, dehydrated

1 tablespoon green onions, dehydrated

1 tablespoon butter powder

1/2 teaspoon cornstarch

1 tablespoon nutritional yeast

1/2 teaspoon garlic powder

1/8 teaspoon thyme

1/8 teaspoon oregano

1/4 teaspoon kosher salt

1/8 teaspoon ground black pepper

1/2 teaspoon (1 packet) crystallized lemon powder

1 tablespoon olive oil

INGREDIENT NOTES

capers: purchase small capers and dehydrate

chicken meatballs: substitute with freeze-dried chicken, or dehydrate canned chicken

crystallized lemon powder: substitute with 1 teaspoon fresh lemon juice (packaged separately)

green onions: slice green onions (white and green parts) and dehydrate

mushrooms: slice white button mushrooms or porcini mushrooms and dehydrate

nutritional yeast: used as a healthy substitute for chicken bouillon

pasta: for better rehydrating, pre-cook pasta and dehydrate or use a pasta that cooks in 5 minutes or less

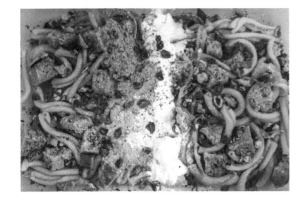

AT HOME

Mix all ingredients together and package in a plastic bag or vacuum seal.

Package olive oil separately.

AT CAMP

Bring 1 cup (8 ounces) of water to a full boil.

Add all of the ingredients and stir well.

Turn the heat to low and simmer for 2 minutes.

Turn off the heat, cover and let sit for 15 minutes until all ingredients are fully rehydrated.

Add olive oil and reheat if needed.

Chipotle Corn Chowder

This smoky corn chowder is full of flavor,
with corn, shredded potatoes, and onions in a creamy base.

difficulty rating ★★☆☆   *recipe by Sanjana*   🌿 *vegetarian*

Nutrition info: calories 416; fat 7g; cholesterol 24mg; sodium 433mg; carbohydrates 53g; protein 9g

Makes 1 serving

INGREDIENTS

1/4 cup corn, dehydrated

1/2 cup shredded potatoes, dehydrated

1/3 cup instant potato flakes

1/2 teaspoon jalapeno, dehydrated (optional)

1 tablespoon chopped onion, dehydrated

1 tablespoon heavy cream powder

1 tablespoon shredded cheddar cheese, freeze-dried

1 teaspoon nutritional yeast

1/4 teaspoon onion powder

1/4 teaspoon chipotle pepper powder

1/8 teaspoon garlic powder

1/4 teaspoon kosher salt

INGREDIENT NOTES

corn: dehydrate canned or frozen corn

jalapeno: if using, chop fresh jalapeno and dehydrate

freeze-dried cheese: substitute with 1 teaspoon cheddar cheese powder

heavy cream powder: whole milk powder can be used in this recipe, but we don't recommend using non-fat or skim milk powder

instant potato flakes: we recommend brands without additives, such as Bob's Red Mill

nutritional yeast: used as a healthy substitute for chicken bouillon

onion: finely dice onion and dehydrate; substitute with dehydrated green onions or purchase dried onion flakes

shredded potatoes: cook whole potatoes and then shred and dehydrate

AT HOME

Mix all ingredients together and package in a plastic bag or vacuum seal.

AT CAMP

Bring 1-1/2 cups (10 ounces) of water to a full boil.

Add dried ingredients and stir well.

Simmer on low heat for 2 minutes.

Turn off heat, cover and let sit for 15 minutes until fully rehydrated.

Reheat if needed.

Fall Harvest Stuffing

This backpacking stuffing recipe – with winter squash and mushrooms – is like having Thanksgiving in the backcountry.

difficulty rating ★★☆☆   *recipe by Lisa*   🍃 *vegetarian*

Nutrition info: calories 538; fat 19g; cholesterol 14mg; sodium 658mg; carbohydrates 51g; protein 13g

Makes 1 serving

INGREDIENTS

1-1/4 cup bread cubes, dried
1/4 cup butternut squash, dehydrated
1/4 cup mushrooms, dehydrated
1/4 cup navy beans, dehydrated
1 tablespoon green onions, dehydrated
1 tablespoon butter powder
1 tablespoon nutritional yeast
1/4 teaspoon onion powder
1/4 teaspoon parsley
1/8 teaspoon garlic powder
1/8 teaspoon thyme
1/8 teaspoon oregano
1/2 teaspoon poultry seasoning
1/2 teaspoon kosher salt
1/4 teaspoon ground black pepper
1 tablespoon olive oil

INGREDIENT NOTES

bread cubes: cut rustic sourdough or multigrain bread into cubes and dehydrate

butternut squash: any type of winter squash can be used; fully cook and cut into small cubes for dehydrating

green onions: slice green onions (white and green parts) and dehydrate

mushrooms: slice white button mushrooms or porcini mushrooms and dehydrate

navy beans: dehydrate fully cooked or canned beans, drained of liquid

nutritional yeast: used as a healthy substitute for chicken bouillon

poultry seasoning: substitute with sage

AT HOME

Mix all ingredients (except bread cubes) together and package in a plastic bag or vacuum seal.

Package bread cubes and olive oil separately.

AT CAMP

Bring 1 cup (8 ounces) of water to a full boil.

Add package of dried ingredients (except bread cubes) and olive oil. Stir well to mix.

Turn off heat, cover and let soak for 10 minutes.

Reheat the mixture, then add bread cubes and stir well to mix. Let sit for 5 minutes.

Loaded Mashed Potatoes

Creamy mashed potatoes are one of the quickest meals to prepare on trail – it's done almost as soon as you add boiling water to it. We like ours with bacon jerky, but dried mushrooms would also work well.

difficulty rating ★☆☆☆   *recipe by Lisa*

Nutrition info: calories 449; fat 21g; cholesterol 74mg; sodium 779mg; carbohydrates 47g; protein 16g

Makes 1 serving

INGREDIENTS

1 cup instant potato flakes

2 tablespoons heavy cream powder

2 teaspoons butter powder

1 tablespoon green onions, dehydrated

1 teaspoon parsley, dried

1/8 teaspoon ground black pepper

1 ounce bacon jerky

INGREDIENT NOTES

bacon jerky: use shelf stable bacon or bacon jerky – dehydrating bacon is not recommended

green onions: slice green onions (white and green parts) and dehydrate

heavy cream powder: whole milk powder can be used instead, but we don't recommend using non-fat or skim milk powder

instant potato flakes: we recommend brands without additives, such as Bob's Red Mill

vegetarian option: instead of bacon, use 1/4 cup dehydrated mushrooms and add 1/4 teaspoon salt

AT HOME

Add all ingredients except bacon jerky to a plastic bag or vacuum seal.

Package bacon jerky separately.

AT CAMP

Heat bacon in pan until hot. Remove and set aside.

Bring 1-1/2 cups (12 ounces) of water to a boil.

Add dry ingredients and stir well.

Turn off heat, cover and let sit for 5 minutes until all ingredients are fully rehydrated.

Add bacon on top.

Mac & Cheese with Pulled Pork

You could buy a box of mac & cheese from the store and cook it on the trail, but this version will not only taste better, you'll be in full control of the quality of the ingredients. And this version tastes waaaay better.

difficulty rating ★★☆☆   *recipe by Lisa*

Nutrition info: calories 402; fat 18g; cholesterol 64mg; sodium 834mg; carbohydrates 26g; protein 18g

Makes 1 serving

INGREDIENTS

2 ounces (2/3 cup) macaroni, dehydrated

1 ounce pulled pork, dried

2 tablespoons heavy cream powder

1 teaspoon butter powder

3 tablespoons cheddar cheese powder

1 tablespoon green onions, dehydrated

1 teaspoon cornstarch

1/8 teaspoon ground black pepper

INGREDIENT NOTES

green onions: slice green onions (white and green parts) and dehydrate

heavy cream powder: whole milk powder can be used instead, but we don't recommend using non-fat or skim milk powder

macaroni: precook macaroni and dehydrate, or substitute pasta that cooks in 5 minutes or less

pulled pork: we recommend Meat Shredz brand; substitute with bacon jerky or freeze-dried ground beef

vegetarian option: instead of pulled pork, use 1/4 cup dehydrated mushrooms and add 1/4 teaspoon salt

AT HOME

Add all ingredients except pulled pork to a plastic bag or vacuum seal.

Package pulled pork separately.

AT CAMP

Bring 1 cup (8 ounces) of water to a full boil.

Add dried ingredients and stir well.

Simmer on low heat for 2 minutes.

Turn off heat, cover and let sit for 15 minutes until pasta is fully rehydrated.

Add pulled pork and stir. Reheat if needed.

If there's too much liquid, simmer uncovered for a few minutes, stirring constantly to prevent burning on the bottom of the pot.

DINNER

Moroccan Stew

*A smoky blend of tomatoes, chickpeas, and sweet potatoes
provides the base for this hearty stew with chicken meatballs.*

difficulty rating ★★★★   *recipe by Sanjana*

Nutrition info: calories 778; fat 26g; cholesterol 61mg; sodium 500mg; carbohydrates 96g; protein 41g

Makes 1 serving

INGREDIENTS

*1/4 cup Moroccan base powder
(see recipe in right column)*

*1/4 cup Asian-style chicken meatballs,
dehydrated (see recipe on page 24)*

1/2 cup chickpeas, dehydrated

2 tablespoons sweet potatoes, dehydrated

1 tablespoon carrot, dehydrated

2 teaspoons cilantro, dehydrated

*1/4 teaspoon (1/2 packet) crystallized
lemon powder*

2 teaspoons olive oil

INGREDIENT NOTES

carrots: dice raw carrots into small pieces
and dehydrate

chickpeas: dehydrate canned or fully cooked
chickpeas

cilantro: dehydrate fresh cilantro or use dried

crystallized lemon powder: substitute with
1 teaspoon fresh lemon juice (packaged
separately)

sweet potatoes: dice raw sweet potatoes; boil
in water for 10 minutes with 1 teaspoon salt;
drain and dehydrate

AT HOME

Mix all ingredients together and package in a
plastic bag or vacuum seal. Package olive oil
separately.

AT CAMP

Bring 1-1/2 cups (12 ounces) of water to a boil.

Add package of dried ingredients and olive oil.
Stir well to mix.

Turn off heat, cover and let soak for
20 minutes. Reheat if needed.

PREPARING THE MOROCCAN BASE

Makes 6 servings

INGREDIENTS

2 teaspoons olive oil

1 large onion, chopped

5 cloves of garlic, chopped

*1 can (24-ounce) fire-roasted crushed
tomato*

15-ounce can chickpeas, drained

2 tablespoons cumin powder

1 teaspoon crushed red pepper (optional)

2 cups chicken broth

DIRECTIONS

Heat oil in a pan. Add onions and garlic and
cook until translucent for 5-7 minutes.

Add cumin powder and red pepper and stir for
a few seconds.

Add tomatoes and chickpeas. Cook for 4-5
minutes longer.

Add the chicken broth. Bring to a boil, then
turn heat to low and simmer for 30 minutes to
reduce the liquid. Turn off heat and let cool for
15 minutes.

Puree the mixture in a blender or food
processor.

Spread the mixture onto dehydrator trays and
dehydrate at 135 degrees until completely dry.

Process the dried base to a powder in a food
processor.

DINNER

Mushroom Stroganoff

Egg noodles and mushrooms are combined with sour cream powder and paprika to make a backpacking spin on traditional stroganoff.

difficulty rating ★★☆☆   *recipe by Lisa*   🌿 *vegetarian*

Nutrition info: calories 542; fat 26g; cholesterol 89mg; sodium 693mg; carbohydrates 61g; protein 14g

Makes 1 serving

INGREDIENTS

2 ounces wide egg noodles, dehydrated

1/2 cup mushrooms, dehydrated

1 tablespoon green onions, dehydrated

1 tablespoon butter powder

2 tablespoons sour cream powder

1/2 teaspoon cornstarch

1/2 teaspoon Hungarian paprika

2 teaspoons parsley, dried

1/4 teaspoon garlic powder

1/2 teaspoon kosher salt

1/8 teaspoon ground black pepper

1 tablespoon olive oil

INGREDIENT NOTES

egg noodles: pre-cook and dehydrate or use noodles that cook in 5 minutes or less

green onions: slice green onions (white and green parts) and dehydrate

mushrooms: slice white button mushrooms or porcini mushrooms and dehydrate

sour cream powder: heavy cream powder or whole milk powder can be used instead, but we don't recommend using non-fat or skim milk powder

DINNER

AT HOME

Mix all ingredients together and package in a plastic bag or vacuum seal.

Package olive oil separately.

AT CAMP

Bring 1 cup (8 ounces) of water to a full boil.

Add dried ingredients and stir well.

Simmer on low heat for 2 minutes.

Turn off heat, cover and let sit for 15 minutes until pasta is fully rehydrated.

Add olive oil and reheat if needed.

Nepali Red Lentils & Rice

This traditional Nepali lentil dish (Dal Bhat) combines red lentils with rice for a creamy and earthy meal.

difficulty rating ★★★☆   *recipe by Sanjana*   🍃 *vegetarian*

Nutrition info: calories 444; fat 25g; cholesterol 27mg; sodium 634mg; carbohydrates 45g; protein 16g

Makes 1 serving

INGREDIENTS

1/2 cup prepared red lentils, dehydrated
(see recipe in right column)

1/2 cup basmati or long grain rice,
dehydrated

2 tablespoons fire-roasted peppers and
onion, dehydrated

1 tablespoon carrots and peas, dehydrated

1 tablespoon spinach, dehydrated

1 tablespoon cauliflower, dehydrated

1/8 teaspoon kosher salt

1 tablespoon (1 packet) ghee

INGREDIENT NOTES

carrots and peas: dehydrate frozen peas and
carrots

cauliflower: pre-cook or use frozen; cut
cauliflower into small florets and dehydrate

fire-roasted peppers and onions: substitute
with dehydrated fresh or frozen bell peppers
and onions

ghee: substitute with an equal amount of
olive oil

lentils: soak lentils for 2 hours and drain
before cooking

spicy option: add 1/2 jalapeno to the lentils

spinach: chop fresh or frozen spinach and
dehydrate

AT HOME

Mix all dried ingredients together and package in
a plastic bag or vacuum seal. Keep ghee packaged
separately.

AT CAMP

Bring 1 cup (8 ounces) of water to a full boil.
Add ingredients and stir well. Turn off heat, cover
and let sit for 15 minutes until fully rehydrated.
Add ghee and stir. Reheat if needed.

PREPARING THE RED LENTILS

Makes 6 servings

INGREDIENTS

1 cup red lentils

1 large yellow onion, chopped

1 large tomato, chopped

2 tablespoons cilantro, chopped

2 large garlic cloves, chopped fine

1 teaspoon cumin seeds

1 teaspoon turmeric powder

1/2 teaspoon red chili powder

1-1/2 teaspoons salt

1 teaspoon olive oil

4 cups water

DIRECTIONS

Heat oil in a pan on medium heat. Add cumin
seeds and lightly toast.

Add garlic, onions and salt. Saute until the
onions are translucent. Add splash of water if
needed to prevent sticking in pan.

Add lentils, spices, tomatoes, and water.
Bring to a boil and simmer on low heat for 30
minutes uncovered. The dish should be a little
thick and not watery.

Turn off heat and add chopped cilantro. Let
it cool, then spread lentils in a thin layer on
dehydrator trays. Dehydrate at 135 degrees
until completely dry.

Penne Puttanesca

*A hearty pasta with the salty tanginess of olives and capers
in a light tomato base, topped with parmesan cheese.*

difficulty rating ★★★☆   *recipe by Sanjana*

Nutrition info: calories 651; fat 27g; cholesterol 46mg; sodium 752mg; carbohydrates 70g; protein 24g

INGREDIENTS

Makes 1 serving

*1 cup pasta base, dehydrated
(see recipe in the right column)*

1/3 cup sausage, freeze-dried

2 tablespoons Parmesan cheese, shredded

1 teaspoon basil, dried

2 teaspoons olive oil

INGREDIENT NOTES

tomatoes: use any type of canned tomatoes:
whole, chopped or crushed

vegetarian option: instead of sausage, use
1/4 cup dehydrated mushrooms

PREPARING THE PASTA BASE

Makes 6 servings

INGREDIENTS

1 pound dry penne pasta, cooked

1 can (28-ounce) chopped tomatoes

*1/2 cup kalamata olives,
pitted and sliced in half*

6 teaspoons capers

1 cup onions, chopped

4 cloves garlic, chopped

1 teaspoon olive oil

1/2 teaspoon crushed red pepper

1 teaspoon salt

DIRECTIONS

Heat oil in a pan and add onions, garlic, and
red pepper. Cool until translucent.

Add tomatoes and cook for 2-3 minutes.

Add cooked penne, olives, and capers.
Simmer for 1-2 minutes and remove from
heat to cool.

Spread pasta mixture in a thin layer on
dehydrator trays. Dehydrate at 135 degrees
until completely dry.

AT HOME

Mix all ingredients together and package in a
plastic bag or vacuum seal. Package olive oil and
Parmesan cheese separately.

AT CAMP

Bring 1 cup (8 ounces) of water to a full boil.

Add all of the ingredients except olive oil and
cheese and stir well.

Turn the heat to low and simmer for 2 minutes.

Turn off the heat, cover, and let sit for 15 minutes
until all ingredients are fully rehydrated. Add olive
oil and Parmesan cheese.

Pesto Pasta

Loaded with veggies, this pesto pasta combines zucchini, sun-dried tomatoes, and mushrooms with fettuccine in a garlicky butter sauce.

difficulty rating ★★☆☆   *recipe by Lisa*   🌿 *vegetarian*

Nutrition info: calories 607; fat 35g; cholesterol 22mg; sodium 746mg; carbohydrates 62g; protein 16g

Makes 1 serving

INGREDIENTS

2 ounces rotini pasta, dehydrated

1/4 cup mushrooms, dehydrated

2 teaspoons green onions, dehydrated

2 teaspoons sun-dried tomatoes, diced

2 tablespoons zucchini, dehydrated

1 tablespoon butter powder

1 tablespoon dried basil

1/2 teaspoon garlic powder

1/2 teaspoon cornstarch

1/2 teaspoon salt

1/8 teaspoon pepper

1 tablespoon parmesan cheese

2 tablespoons olive oil

INGREDIENT NOTES

green onions: slice green onions (white and green parts) and dehydrate

mushrooms: slice white button mushrooms or porcini mushrooms and dehydrate

Parmesan cheese powder: add at the end of cooking to prevent sticking to the pan

rotini pasta: for best results, pre-cook the pasta and dehydrate it, or use pasta that cook in 5 minutes or less

sun-dried tomatoes: purchase sun-dried tomatoes that are not packed in oil

zucchini: slice into quarters and dehydrate

AT HOME

Mix all ingredients together and package in a plastic bag or vacuum seal.

Package olive oil and Parmesan cheese separately.

AT CAMP

Bring 1 cup (8 ounces) of water to a full boil.

Add dried ingredients and stir well.

Simmer on low heat for 2 minutes.

Turn off heat, cover and let sit for 15 minutes until pasta is fully rehydrated.

Add olive oil and parmesan cheese and stir to incorporate. If there's too much liquid, simmer uncovered for a few minutes, stirring constantly to prevent burning on the bottom of the pot.

Pineapple & Pork Fried Rice

*This Pacific-island influenced dish combines pulled pork
and pineapple with zucchini, mushrooms, and carrots
for a sweet and savory take on fried rice.*

difficulty rating ★★★☆   recipe by Lisa

Nutrition info: calories 433; fat 15g; cholesterol 30mg; sodium 642mg; carbohydrates 59g; protein 17g

Makes 1 serving

INGREDIENTS

1/2 cup dehydrated Basmati rice

1 ounce Pacific Island-style pulled pork, dehydrated (see recipe in right column)

1/2 ounce pineapple, dehydrated

2 tablespoons zucchini, dehydrated

1 tablespoon green onions, dehydrated

1 tablespoon mushrooms, dehydrated

1 tablespoon carrots, dehydrated

1 teaspoon cornstarch

1 teaspoon soy sauce

1 tablespoon sesame oil

INGREDIENT NOTES

basmati rice: pre-cook and dehydrate; substitute with long grain rice if needed

carrots: shred and dehydrate

green onions: slice green onions (white and green parts) and dehydrate

pineapple: dehydrate canned crushed pineapple

pulled pork: substitute with dried pulled pork (we recommend Meat Shredz brand)

mushrooms: slice white button mushrooms or porcini mushrooms and dehydrate

zucchini: slice into quarters and dehydrate

AT HOME

Mix all ingredients together and package in a plastic bag or vacuum seal.

Package soy sauce and sesame oil separately.

AT CAMP

Bring 3/4 cup (6 ounces) of water to a boil.

Add all ingredients and stir well.

Simmer on low heat for 2 minutes.

Turn off heat and let sit for 15 minutes.

Reheat if needed.

PACIFIC ISLAND-STYLE PULLED PORK

Makes 8 servings

INGREDIENTS

1 pound pork tenderloin

1 can (15 ounce) crushed pineapple

2 tablespoons soy sauce

1/2 teaspoon garlic powder

2 tablespoons onion, chopped

DIRECTIONS

Place all ingredients in a slow cooker and cook for 6 hours. Shred with a fork into small pieces. Spread thin on dehydrator trays and dehydrate at 155 degrees until fully dry.

DINNER

Quinoa Lentil Stew

This earthy stew combines lentils and quinoa with green beans, carrots, and peas in a tomato curry sauce.

difficulty rating ★★★☆   *recipe by Sanjana*   🌿 *vegetarian*

Nutrition info: calories 736; fat 18g; cholesterol 0mg; sodium 399mg; carbohydrates 118g; protein 33g

Makes 1 serving

INGREDIENTS

2 tablespoons tomato curry base, dehydrated
(see recipe on page 25)

1/2 cup brown lentils, cooked, dehydrated

1/2 cup cooked quinoa, dehydrated

1 tablespoon frozen green beans, dehydrated

1 tablespoon carrots, dehydrated

1 tablespoon peas, dehydrated

2 tablespoons coconut milk powder

5 curry leaves, dried, crushed

1/2 teaspoon cumin powder

1/8 teaspoon garlic powder

1/4 teaspoon kosher salt

1/2 tablespoon dried coconut chips for
topping

INGREDIENT NOTES

carrots: dice carrots, boil for 10 minutes, drain
and dehydrate (or use frozen carrot pieces)

cilantro: dehydrate whole stalks with leaves or
use dried cilantro

coconut milk powder: whole milk powder may
be used instead, but non-fat milk powder is not
recommended

green beans: dehydrate canned or frozen
French-style green beans

lentils: soak 1 cup brown lentils for 4 hours and
drain. Add 4 cups of water, lentils, 1/2 teaspoon
kosher salt in a 1 quart pan. Bring it to a boil and
then simmer for 15-20 minutes. Drain lentils and
dehydrate.

peas: dehydrate frozen petite peas

quinoa: pre-cook quinoa according to package
Directions, then dehydrate

AT HOME

Mix all ingredients together and
package in a plastic bag or vacuum
seal.

Package coconut chips separately.

AT CAMP

Bring 1 cup (8 ounces) of water
to a boil.

Add package of dried ingredients.
Stir well to mix.

Turn off heat, cover and let soak
for 15 minutes.

Top with coconut chips.

Reheat if needed.

DINNER

Salmon Chowder

Salmon chowder is a creamy delight anytime, but especially when camping in colder temps. This recipe uses canned salmon and shredded potatoes that you dehydrate at home, and adds instant mashed potatoes for a thick and creamy chowder.

difficulty rating ★★☆☆   *recipe by Lisa*

Nutrition info: calories 515; fat 29g; cholesterol 86mg; sodium 552mg; carbohydrates 36g; protein 14g

Makes 1 serving

INGREDIENTS

3/4 cup instant potato flakes

1/4 cup shredded potatoes, dehydrated

1/4 cup canned salmon, dehydrated

2 tablespoons heavy cream powder

1 tablespoon butter powder

1 tablespoon green onions, dehydrated

1/8 teaspoon paprika

1/2 teaspoon kosher salt

1/8 teaspoon ground black pepper

1 tablespoon olive oil

INGREDIENT NOTES

green onions: slice green onions (white and green parts) and dehydrate

heavy cream powder: whole milk powder can be used in this recipe, but we don't recommend using non-fat or skim milk powder

instant potato flakes: we recommend brands without additives, such as Bob's Red Mill

salmon: boneless and skinless canned salmon works best for dehydrating

shredded potatoes: cook whole potatoes, shred using a box grater and dehydrate

AT HOME

Mix all ingredients together and package in a plastic bag or vacuum seal.

AT CAMP

Bring 2 cups (16 ounces) of water to a full boil.

Add all ingredients (except olive oil) and stir well.

Turn off the heat and let sit for 15 minutes to fully rehydrate the salmon and shredded potatoes.

Add olive oil and reheat if needed.

DINNER

Spaghetti & Meatballs

Instead of dehydrating pre-made marinara sauce, this version uses dehydrated tomato sauce with garlic, basil, oregano, and meatballs for a fresher take on this Italian classic.

difficulty rating ★★★☆   recipe by Lisa

Nutrition info: calories 546; fat 24g; cholesterol 66mg; sodium 844mg; carbohydrates 60g; protein 24g

Makes 1 serving

INGREDIENTS

2 ounces spaghetti, dehydrated

3 beef meatballs (24 cut pieces), dehydrated (see recipe on page 22)

1 ounce tomato sauce leather

1 tablespoon green onions, dehydrated

1/2 teaspoon garlic powder

1/2 teaspoon basil, dried

1/2 teaspoon oregano, dried

1/8 teaspoon ground black pepper

1 tablespoon Parmesan cheese powder

1 tablespoon olive oil

INGREDIENT NOTES

green onions: slice green onions (white and green parts) and dehydrate

Parmesan cheese powder: add at the end of cooking to prevent sticking to the pan

spaghetti: for better rehydrating, pre-cook the spaghetti and dehydrate, or use a pasta that cooks in 5 minutes or less

tomato leather: spread tomato sauce in a thin layer on silicone or plastic dehydrator trays and dehydrate at 125 degrees for 8-10 hours; or substitute with 1 tablespoon tomato powder

vegetarian option: instead of meatballs, use 1/4 cup dehydrated mushrooms and add 1/4 teaspoon salt

AT HOME

Mix all ingredients together and package in a plastic bag or vacuum seal.

Package olive oil and Parmesan cheese powder separately.

AT CAMP

Bring 1 cup (8 ounces) of water to a boil.

Add all ingredients except olive oil and Parmesan cheese powder and stir well.

Simmer on low for 2 minutes.

Add olive oil, turn off heat, cover and let sit for 15 minutes. Add Parmesan cheese powder just before eating.

Thai Red Curry Noodle Soup

*This spicy noodle soup with chicken meatballs is packed
with flavor from red curry paste, coconut milk powder,
Thai basil, and kaffir lime leaves.*

difficulty rating ★★★☆   *recipe by Sanjana*

Nutrition info: calories 526; fat 32g; cholesterol 57mg; sodium 528mg; carbohydrates 36g; protein 20g

Makes 1 serving

INGREDIENTS

1/2 cup Asian chicken meatballs, dehydrated (see recipe on page 24)

1-1/2 ounces thin rice vermicelli noodles

1 tablespoon green onions, dehydrated

1 tablespoon mushrooms, dehydrated

1 tablespoon shredded carrots, dehydrated

1/2 teaspoon red curry paste, dehydrated, powdered

1/2 teaspoon (1 packet) crystallized lime powder

1 tablespoon Thai basil leaves, dehydrated

1/2 teaspoon kaffir lime leaves, dehydrated

3 tablespoons coconut milk powder

1/4 teaspoon Red Boat salt

INGREDIENT NOTES

carrots: shred fresh carrots and dehydrate

green onions: slice green onions (white and green parts) and dehydrate

kaffir lime leaves: dehydrate whole leaves and then crush into small pieces

mushrooms: slice mushrooms and dehydrate

red curry paste: use any prepared Thai curry paste without oil (Ma Ploy is a recommended brand) and dehydrate, then pulse in a food processor to make a powder; or substitute with red curry powder

Red Boat salt: substitute with 1/2 teaspoon soy sauce (packaged separately)

rice noodles: use thin rice noodles for the best results

Thai basil leaves: dehydrate whole stalks of basil leaves until dry, then remove the leaves from the stems

AT HOME

Mix all ingredients together and package in a plastic bag or vacuum seal.

AT CAMP

Bring 1-1/2 cups (12 ounces) of water to a full boil.

Add all ingredients and stir well.

Turn off the heat and let sit for 20 minutes to fully rehydrate.

Reheat if needed.

Wild Mushroom Risotto

This creamy risotto is full of unami flavor, with wild mushrooms, roasted garlic, rosemary, and Parmesan cheese.

difficulty rating ★★★☆   *recipe by Sanjana*

Nutrition info: calories 726; fat 33g; cholesterol 116mg; sodium 633mg; carbohydrates 77g; protein 18g

Makes 1 serving

INGREDIENTS

*3/4 cup prepared risotto, dehydrated
(see recipe in right column)*

2 tablespoons heavy cream powder

1 tablespoon butter powder

2 tablespoons Parmesan cheese, shredded

INGREDIENT NOTES

heavy cream powder: whole milk powder
can be used in this recipe, but we don't
recommend using non-fat or skim milk powder

mushrooms: use dried wild mushroom mix and
soak in hot water for 20 minutes, then chop
into bite size pieces

AT HOME

Mix all ingredients together and package in a
plastic bag or vacuum seal.

Package Parmesan cheese separately.

AT CAMP

Bring 1 cup (8 ounces) of water to a boil.

Add all ingredients except Parmesan cheese and
stir well. Simmer on low for 2 minutes.

Turn off heat, cover and let sit for 20 minutes. Add
Parmesan cheese just before eating.

PREPARING THE RISOTTO

Makes 5 servings

INGREDIENTS

2-1/2 cups arborio rice

1-1/2 ounces wild mushrooms, dried

3/4 cup shredded Parmesan cheese

1-1/2 teaspoon roasted garlic powder

1 tablespoon rosemary, chopped

1 teaspoon mushroom powder, unsalted

6 tablespoons butter powder

3/4 cup heavy cream powder

4 cups chicken stock, low sodium

1 cup white wine

1 teaspoon kosher salt

DIRECTIONS

In a heavy pan, add stock, rice, mushrooms,
garlic and mushroom powder. Bring to a boil,
then reduce heat and cover. Let simmer for
15 minutes.

Remove lid and stir continuously until most
of the liquid evaporates for a few minutes.
Add rosemary.

Spread in a thin layer on dehydrator
trays and dehydrate at 135 degrees until
completely dry.

Crumble dehydrated mix.

DINNER

Zucchini & Roasted Red Pepper Soup

*Roasted red bell peppers and zucchini are combined
with coconut milk powder for a rich and flavorful soup.*

difficulty rating ★★★☆   *recipe by Sanjana*   🌿 *vegetarian*

Nutrition info: calories 313; fat 21g; cholesterol 0mg; sodium 492mg; carbohydrates 33g; protein 5g

Makes 1 serving

INGREDIENTS

1/4 cup zucchini-pepper base, dehydrated

3 tablespoons coconut milk powder

1 tablespoon sun-dried tomatoes

mini toasts or crackers for topping

INGREDIENT NOTES

coconut milk powder: whole milk powder may be used instead, but non-fat milk powder is not recommended

nutritional yeast: used as a healthy substitute for chicken bouillon

sun-dried tomatoes: purchase sun-dried tomatoes that are not packed in oil

PREPARING THE ZUCCHINI & RED PEPPER BASE

Makes 4 servings

INGREDIENTS

1-1/2 pounds zucchini, diced

1 large yellow onion, diced

6 cloves garlic, chopped

2 cups roasted red bell peppers, diced

2 teaspoons nutritional yeast

1/4 teaspoon onion powder

2 teaspoons coriander powder

1/2 teaspoon kosher salt

2 teaspoons olive oil

2 cups water

DIRECTIONS

In a 2-quart heavy pan, heat 2 teaspoons of olive oil.

Add garlic and stir for a few seconds. Add onions and salt. Sauté for 5-6 minutes until translucent.

Add zucchini, diced roasted red peppers, coriander powder, nutritional yeast, onion powder, and 2 cups of water. Let simmer for 20-25 minutes.

Cool. Puree in a blender.

Pour onto dehydrator trays lined with silicone or plastic trays. Dehydrate at 125 degrees until completely dry.

Process in a food processor to convert to a powder.

AT HOME

Mix all ingredients together and package in a plastic bag or vacuum seal.

AT CAMP

Bring 1-1/4 cups (10 ounces) of water to a boil.

Add package of dried ingredients. Stir well to mix.

Turn off the heat and let sit for 15 minutes to fully rehydrate. Reheat if needed.

Top with crackers or mini toast.

Apple Crisp

Combining tart apples with crunchy granola and heavy cream powder gives this apple crisp a fresh baked flavor.

difficulty rating ★☆☆☆   *recipe by Lisa*   🌿 *vegetarian*

Nutrition info: calories 326; fat 6g; cholesterol 15mg; sodium 80mg; carbohydrates 63g; protein 5g

Makes 1 serving

INGREDIENTS

1/2 cup dehydrated apple pieces

1 tablespoon heavy cream powder

1 tablespoon cane sugar

1/2 teaspoon cornstarch

1/8 teaspoon cinnamon

1/2 cup + 2 tablespoons plain granola

INGREDIENT NOTES

apples: chop fresh apples into 1/2" pieces and dehydrate; any combination of the following will work in this recipe: dehydrated peaches, nectarines, or apricots; freeze-dried blueberries, strawberries or raspberries

cinnamon: Saigon cinnamon works well in this recipe; or substitute ground ginger or a smaller amount of nutmeg

granola: any type of whole oats granola can be used in this recipe; we recommend Bob's Red Mill brand

heavy cream powder: coconut milk powder or whole milk powder can be used instead, but we don't recommend using non-fat or skim milk powders

AT HOME

Mix all ingredients (except 2 tablespoons granola) together and package in a plastic bag or vacuum seal.

Store 2 tablespoons granola in a separate bag.

AT CAMP

Bring 1/2 cup (4 ounces) water to a boil.

Place ingredients in a pan or plastic jar with a lid.

Add water and stir.

Cover and let sit for 15 minutes.

Add additional granola before eating.

DESSERT

Chocolate-Orange Pudding

Dark, rich, creamy chocolate pudding with crispy oranges and sea salt topping is a luxurious dessert in the backcountry that's easy to prepare.

difficulty rating ★★☆☆   *recipe by Sanjana*   🌱 *vegetarian*

Nutrition info: calories 222; fat 5g; cholesterol 0mg; sodium 310mg; carbohydrates 47g; protein 5g

Makes 1 serving

INGREDIENTS

3 tablespoons cocoa powder

1 tablespoon whole milk powder

1-1/2 tablespoons instant gel powder

2 tablespoons sugar

1/4 teaspoon vanilla powder

1/8 teaspoon sea salt flakes

2 orange slices, dehydrated

INGREDIENT NOTES

cocoa powder: use a high quality cocoa powder with no additives for best results

instant gel powder: use instant clear gel, not the type that needs to be cooked

milk powder: coconut milk powder can be used instead, but we don't recommend using non-fat or skim milk powders

orange slices: remove orange peel and pith, thinly slice; dehydrate; break into smaller pieces

AT HOME

Mix all ingredients (except orange slices and sea salt flakes) together and package in a plastic bag or vacuum seal.

Package orange slices and sea salt flakes separately.

AT CAMP

Empty package of dried ingredients into a bowl, pan or mug.

Add 1/2 cup (4 ounces) of cold water.

Stir well until it thickens.

Add orange slice pieces and sea salt on top.

DESSERT

Ginger Creme Brulee

Wow your campmates by whipping up this easy yet decadent dessert that's creamy and full-flavored with candied ginger and a caramelized sugar topping. Don't forget to share!

difficulty rating ★★☆☆   *recipe by Sanjana*   🌿 *vegetarian*

Nutrition info: calories 427; fat 11g; cholesterol 133mg; sodium 153mg; carbohydrates 68g; protein 12g

Makes 1 serving

INGREDIENTS

1/4 cup whole milk powder

2 tablespoons instant clear gel powder

1 tablespoon whole egg powder

2 tablespoons sugar

2 teaspoons chopped crystallized ginger

1 teaspoon vanilla powder

1/8 teaspoon turmeric powder (for color)

1/8 teaspoon cinnamon powder

Caramelized Topping:

1 tablespoon sugar

1 teaspoon water

INGREDIENT NOTES

egg powder: purchase dried whole egg powder instead of dehydrating cooked eggs

instant gel powder: use instant clear gel, not the type that needs to be cooked

milk powder: coconut milk powder can be used instead, but we don't recommend using non-fat or skim milk powders

AT HOME

Caramelized sugar topping: Place sugar with water in a small heavy stainless-steel pan and bring it to a boil. Let boil until the color just begins to turn light brown. Remove from heat and pour on a silicone mat or parchment paper. Cool and then break into small chunks. Pack in a small plastic bag.

Mix the remaining ingredients together and package in a plastic bag or vacuum seal.

AT CAMP

Empty package of dried ingredients into a bowl, pan or mug.

Add 1/2 cup (4 ounces) of cold water.

Mix continuously for 1-2 minutes, until fully dissolved without any lumps.

Let sit for 5 minutes.

Top with the caramelized sugar pieces.

Mango Rice Pudding

This rich and creamy rice pudding is studded with mango and almonds and cooks up quick at camp for an easy dessert.

difficulty rating ★★★☆   recipe by Sanjana   🌿 vegetarian

Nutrition info: calories 443; fat 20g; cholesterol 28mg; sodium 186mg; carbohydrates 71g; protein 14g

Makes 1 serving

INGREDIENTS

*1/4 cup dehydrated rice mixture
(see recipe in the right column)*

2 tablespoons whole milk powder

1 tablespoon raw almonds

1/2 tablespoon dried mango

1-1/2 tablespoons brown sugar

INGREDIENT NOTES

almond slices: substitute finely chopped almonds

short grain sticky rice: sometimes also labeled as sweet rice or glutenous rice

whole milk powder: coconut milk powder can be used instead, but non-fat milk powder is not recommended

AT HOME

Mix all ingredients together and package in a plastic bag or vacuum seal.

AT CAMP

Empty contents with 3/4 cup water (6 ounces) into a pan and bring to a boil.

Stir constantly to avoid burning on the bottom of the pan.

Cover and let sit for 10 minutes.

PREPARING THE RICE

Makes 6 servings

INGREDIENTS

1 cup short grain sticky rice

4 cups almond milk

3/4 cup whole milk powder

1/2 cup brown sugar

1/2 cup almond slices

1/2 cup dried mango, chopped

1 teaspoon cardamom powder

pinch saffron (optional)

DIRECTIONS

Bring almond milk, saffron, and rice to a simmer for 10-15 minutes. Stir continuously until rice is fully cooked.

Spread rice thinly onto dehydrator trays.

Dehydrate at 135 degrees until completely dry, turning over partway through the drying time.

Coarsely chop dried rice mixture in a food processor.

Index

The **I Heart Pacific Northwest** website is a companion guide to this book, featuring a detailed list of recommended backpacking gear, trip reports, gear reviews, and how-to info.

iheartpacificnorthwest.com

CPSIA information can be obtained
at www.ICGtesting.com
Printed in the USA
BVHW021922200222
629613BV00002B/6